A J

to

Kurdistan

• • • • • • • • • • •

Ruwayda Mustafah

IBN-13: 978-1512135886

CreateSpace, a DBA of On-Demand Publishing, LLC.

Designed by Ibrahim Desoky.

ACKNOWLEDGMENTS

To my father, Mustafah Rabar, who instilled the
love of literature in me, and believed in my dreams
when others doubted me.

This page was intentionally left blank.

CONTENTS

FORWARD

Polly Trout, Ph.D.
Seattle, WA
April 9, 2013.

One of the joys of my current job is that I have the honour of meeting young immigrant women from all over the world, college students who are ferociously passionate about education and social justice. They open up new worlds and ideas to me, and trying to keep up with them keeps me young at heart. Each of their stories is different, as different as their homelands – Gambia, Mongolia, Mexico, Guatemala, India, Yemen, Russia, Ethiopia, the Philippines. Collectively, however, their stories invariably circle back to shared and universal themes of identity, survival, resilience, autonomy and community. Journey to Kurdistan is an example of this emerging international genre of feminist autobiography for a new generation.

Ruwayda Mustafah Rabar was born in 1989 in the city of Erbil (also known as Hewlêr) in Kurdistan Region. Erbil is one of the oldest continually inhabited cities in the world. At age eleven, Ruwayda moved with her family to London, where she embraced her new life as a British citizen, eventually attending university where an unrealised interest in feminism and activism was sparked. Regular family visits to Kurdistan maintained a connection to her homeland, which she investigated in more detail in 2012. Following graduation from law school, Ruwayda lived in Kurdistan for more than a year, documenting her work as an anthropological researcher, interviewing women about their lives and beliefs.

This memoir combines autobiography, travelogue, ethnography, philosophy, and cultural criticism. As Ruwayda comes of age, she discovers an identity developed amid conflicting cultural and traditional loyalties. What does it mean to be a woman? A Muslim? A Kurd? A citizen of the world? A feminist? An activist? How can these conflicting identities be harmonised within one individual in a way that is powerful and authentic? This book intentionally asks questions that might only be answered in additional memoirs – perhaps when Ruwayda is 43, 63, or 93 her personal growth and experience will enable her to cast a critical eye over issues that right now seem immutable.

Journey to Kurdistan is more than a memoir: it is a call to action, a polemic that rejects gender-based oppression and unapologetically promotes a worldview where men and women share power and opportunity in a society organised primarily by cooperation rather than coercion. Ruwayda celebrates her identity as a Muslim woman and a Kurd, but demands that she be primarily recognised as a human being and a thinker. It is this determined insistence on the universality of human dignity and worth that makes the book glow with such warmth. For those who feebly caricature feminism as nothing more than the hatred of men, this book makes it clear that feminists are struggling for a better future for all human beings, not just women - we are all connected and we rise or fall together.

I am now in my forties, and my daughters are 10 and 12. I worry about their fate; sometimes it seems as if things are getting worse for women, rather than better, despite generations of struggle for women's rights. When I'm feeling down, my youngest daughter says, "Don't worry, Mama. Your generation screwed things up pretty bad, but my generation will fix it." It gives me hope to imagine that all over the world, courageous young women like Ruwayda will be there to guide and mentor my daughters in carrying on that good fight. The more we can listen to each other, learn from each other, and cooperate with each other, the sooner we will triumph, and finally create a world where all girls can grow up to be strong, independent, safe, and free.

PREFACE

I wrote this book in an unusual manner. I wrote much of it while interviewing people and edited it later. I scribbled on my notepad, phone or iPad, sometimes on a bus journey home or a train, but mostly I wrote at a coffee shop on London's Putney High Street, during my time as an undergraduate. The aroma of the coffee, background chitchat and convenient (*free!*) wireless service were a haven for me when I needed a break from the rigours of law school.

A journey to Kurdistan is a voyage to a region until recently unknown to much of the world. Slowly, the outline of Kurdistan is being recognised on the global map. Here you will find my reflections of Kurdistan, its growing economy and dependence on others. Although I present my thoughts in many sections, the primary discussion running throughout is the need for social and economic freedom.

Kurdish people have relied on others for a long time, a practice rooted in cultural tradition. For much of our lives we depend on our parents, regardless of any financial independence we may establish as adults, and we maintain this dependence throughout our lives.

This book aims to give people a glimpse into the many aspects of Kurdish culture, at once enlightening and unveiling the full extent of societal problems. This work, however, is not a complete authority of Kurdish culture; it merely explores an area with abundant opportunity for development. During my research I have been fortunate to meet people who have shared their insight about Kurdistan and human nature. To respect privacy I have changed names in the stories you will read.

This book began with a personal journey to Kurdistan that grew to include meaning far greater than my personal desire to seek answers. In the summer of 2012 I interviewed several people in the region and methodically compiled the notes which became the basis of this work. My constant companions during my travels throughout cities and remote villages were a scribbled notepad and well-keyed mobile phone.

Kurdistan, or the vast area in which Kurdish people have traditionally lived, is a region encompassing parts of Iran, Iraq, Syria and Turkey. The history of the Kurdish struggle for autonomy has received more attention in recent times. While the independence of the Kurdish people is of great importance to me, here you will read mostly my reflections of the inner struggles taking place in Southern Kurdistan — the place of my birth.

Southern Kurdistan has experienced unprecedented growth in the last decade. Yet this growth has not bought about change in some of the more problematic aspects of Kurdish society. The way social structures work to undermine women's advancement, for example, and how a fragmented economy is cementing class divisions in the region.

Despite the rise of a small elite, these social ills — namely the lack of female leadership, the increasing poverty of the poor and the neglect of orphaned children — remain omnipresent in the region. A Journey to Kurdistan exposes these social problems with the main goal of promoting humane and inclusive progress for everyone. That said, I must declare outright that I am not an expert of Kurdish history and merely having Kurdish ancestry does not make me an authority on Kurdish matters. I am simply a person following a moral obligation to seek justice and respect humanity.

My effort to answer the call for action was made possible by the involvement of several people who opened their homes and hearts to me, and who took the time to consider my questions and answer them with poignant honesty. To these generous people I remain grateful and indebted. As you embark on your own journey to Kurdistan, you will come to know many of these brave souls. Although many names have been changed to safeguard privacy, I hope this will not interfere with your ability to connect with their stories on a human level.

Honest observation on this journey has brought me enemies and few friends because, like people everywhere, Kurds do not appreciate what they perceive as criticism of their motherland. As Kurdish readers take in some parts of this book, they may express concern with how it represents them — they do not wish it to project a negative image of Kurdish people. So let me be clear: the Kurds are vastly different, depending on which community, city or neighbourhood they are from.

The information presented here combines stories, informal reports of events, observations and general analysis. My choice to write honestly about what I have seen in Kurdistan has angered some people, offended others and at times earned me the reputation of cultural traitor. I do not take this to heart because I understand that many of the improvements needed in Kurdistan require a thorough reevaluation of the unethical aspects of culture. For example, if a married woman develops a close relationship with another man and later meets her death at the hands of relatives defending honour, surely this is a tradition that we — as human beings — must speak about and challenge. If children labour long hours at street markets and beg on street corners in the cold of winter because their parents are too poor to survive without the extra income, we must bear witness to their plight. The choice to speak the truth — and not shield it from public knowledge in the name of cultural guardianship — is one that makes us human and adds value to a truly honourable experience in the world.

In the same vein, we must remember that there is a great deal of good in Kurdish society, and there are many Kurdish people who support global progress. Like most places on Earth, Southern Kurdistan is fraught with good and evil, beaming with endless possibility for advancement. To seize this opportunity we must side with honesty and cooperation. There are countless young women in the region who are cementing change into the societal fabric.

For instance, the number of young Kurdish women actively trying to change the very nature of patriarchy in the region has been steadily increasing in the past decade. Take for instance, **Biza Barzo**, a young Kurdish woman who has participated in numerous campaigns to help fundraise for families of Peshmerga continues to be a glimmer of hope. She is currently running for the post of presidency within the American University of Slemani-Iraq, and I hope one day she will be a leader of an independent Kurdistan.

It's not just Biza, but there are many young women with bright ideas to change societal attitudes towards various things. Mostly recently, **_Nuha Serrac_** modelled in a series of pictures to highlight the horrific nature of domestic violence. Her pictures were used on various social networking sites to highlight the gruesome nature and reality of violence. The pictures depicted several violent marks on her face and body, it raised an important issue in our society where domestic violence is rarely seen in the public eye and mainstream discourse.

Nuha has also initiated a public campaign to keep our cities clean, and in the past worked on dozens of projects to help the region blossom and progress into a better democracy. We have many young activists, such as **_Ashna Shareff_**, an aspiring poet, paving the ways towards a better society. The list of young women in the region is long, but I want to highlight some of them because they're an important part of our society.

Delal Sindy, a Swedish-Kurdish woman returned to Kurdistan Region as a volunteer to help refugees and internally displaced people. She has helped Yazidi women by documenting their sufferings under the brutal captivity of Islamic State militants in Iraq and Syria. Similarly, *Taffan Ako Taha* has volunteered to assist refugees in the region, bringing their voices into an international platform.

It's not just returnees from the West that are cementing change within our communities, but many young locals such as *Dastan Haji Othman*, a young Kurdish girl who invented a bomb-detection device in secondary school, alongside *Eman Abdul-Razzaq Ibrahim*. These two young girls have inspired many in the region to excel in various fields, and not just areas that are traditionally believed to be where young women should campaign or be active.

A young mother, and local Blogger *Sazan Mandalawi*, is another familiar name, writing about the various elements of Kurdistan region through her lenses. To the orphans in Erbil city, she is a familiar face, one that many young children in the orphanage have loved and earnestly sought her counsel.

Our young women are not only diverse, but each one of them are pursuing a path to make the region better. Together, they're an unbreakable force of good, despite having differences of opinion. Their belief in making Kurdistan better unites them. You will see them supporting each other in campaigns, endorsing one another publicly, and providing many young women in the region with hope in a better future.

ROOTS

"A people without knowledge of their history, origin and culture is like a tree without roots."

Marcus Garvey

When I was a teenager, the huge vacuum of information about who Kurdish people were left me feeling as if I had no roots. Unlike today, when I was growing up very few Kurdish people were using social networks, which hindered diaspora communities from forging ties. Of course no one can destroy Kurdish culture, but if we don't know about it, and stop reading, learning, exploring our roots, we inevitably destroy it. Kurdish culture is unique; it encompasses various religions and is influenced by the diversity of its neighbours, but despite this, few are fascinated by the rich history of our heritage, instead more fixated with a sense of nationalism.

In modern day Kurdistan, Western values are absorbed, partially because of globalisation and improved access to the internet. This transformation has radically altered the local demand for products and the region's infrastructure. The influx of ideas penetrating Kurdish culture has created a multidimensional struggle between religion, politics, progress and globalisation.

This has been especially true since the fall of Saddam Hussein in 2003, which motivated thinkers to rescue Kurdish culture from the grip of extremists — people who want to preserve the archaic aspects of Kurdish culture and destroy the rich components of our heritage. Since the emergence of the "Islamic State" in 2014, headed by Abu Bakr al-Baghdadi, and its militant followers, the Kurdistan Region has been on high alert, as it once more faces a tyrannical militarised threat.

Kurdish people have struggled for autonomy since the early 20th century. During the Saddam Hussein regime they were the target of a genocidal campaign and forced to assimilate in several cities. Systematic discrimination had effectively prevented Kurds from forming political parties, but this changed with the fall of Saddam and the Iraq war. Now the Kurdistan Region is experiencing rapid growth in political and communications systems. Kurds have formed new political parties and established a variety of media channels. These developments have also brought challenges as not all people are ready for the advances that facilitate globalisation. But in reality all stages of development present obstacles that people must overcome — culture is ever-changing and progress invariably transforms old customs.

The Kurdistan Region is progressing. However, despite this progress, the voices of the poor and disadvantaged remain suppressed. Instead of helping the needy, the privileged few are part of a systematic oppression. Those who have always lived in the Kurdistan Region's capital, Erbil and surrounding areas may not notice the changes over the years; but for people who live periodically in the city, the changing social fabric is highly visible.

There are young activists in the Kurdistan Region. However, this group is over-represented by those from privileged backgrounds or Western Kurds that have returned to the motherland, having experienced, and continuing to enjoy, greater freedom. This is not to say, locals are not as active, but returnees from foreign countries are more able to exploit the abundance of opportunities available to them.

Kurdistan is experiencing a transitory phase, and if the young people of today are to successfully lead the region in the future, the current leadership must acknowledge social problems. Governmental institutions that assist people must be established. Political and social structures that characterise women as inferior to men must be revised. Real leaders must display the courage to challenge dehumanising practices that are motivated by what is considered as honourable.

Honour is a driving force that transcends financial and social status throughout Kurdistan, where people like to apply honour in all situations. Patriarchal values feature prominently in expressions of honour. Thus even in families where power rests in the hands of women, it usually derives from patriarchal ideals. As we discuss honour, I suggest we avoid generalisations or an inflexible judgment that throws all Kurds in a common pool. People everywhere are full of complexities, and judging an entire ethnic group based on a bad custom is neither constructive nor honest. Nonetheless, we should not disregard aspects of our culture that are backward, for the sake of perpetuating an ideal that does not exist in reality.

What many fail to realise is that the notion of "honour" or "honourable practices" is deeply rooted throughout the Middle East, and not just Kurdistan. In fact, although codes of "honour" subtly exist in the Kurdistan Region, neighbouring countries face the grit of its practices far more severely and brutally.

Not all Kurdish families follow traditions in a way that limit their horizons, as has been depicted by orientalist perceptions of Kurds for decades. My family, for example, appreciate Kurdish culture, but remain receptive to new ideas. Their acceptance of my desire to travel and to mingle among the company of those that please me, are largely accepted by them, and other Kurdish parents are as tolerant.

Although my parents incorporated elements of honour in my upbringing, they always emphasised the value of autonomy — at least that is how I recall my own upbringing. I know many other Kurdish families who combine traditional and modern values to maintain a healthy balance in their lives. These are not the people I worry about; I am most concerned about young people from lower and middle-class families — this is the group that suffers most under archaic notions of honour, as I observed first-hand during months of interviews and fieldwork in Kurdistan. Although the number of honour-based cases has reduced drastically in the past decade, nonetheless they still exist throughout the Middle East, and unfortunately in the Kurdistan Region.

We have reached a stage where we are still trying to understand our roots because our culture is faced with change on a massive scale. For centuries we were victims of ourselves, neighbours, the international community, foes and friends, but because of new ways of communicating we have addressed those hindrances and been able to break down walls of oppression through collaboration.

The Kurdistan Region is no longer represented by shallow depictions of its enemies and oppressors. I have found that our voices are finally being heard, we are champions of our rights and leaders in the world. And it is only de règle to convey the region as discovered through my eyes, an informal introduction of a region through the eyes of a girl, a woman, a mother, an activist and more.

FEMINIST REVOLUTION

"Feminism isn't simply about being a woman in a position of power. It's battling systematic inequities; it's a social justice movement that believes sexism, racism and classism exist and interconnect, and that they should be consistently challenged."

Jessica Valenti

Kurdish women patiently await their feminist revolution. Small scale campaigns have made some noise, but still have a long way to go in the struggle for equal rights in the Kurdistan Region, where female leadership is scarce. Nonetheless, since the fall of Saddam, the Kurdistan Region has prospered tremendously, and this has influenced gender relations. Local prosperity has allowed Kurdish women more freedom and job opportunities, making them more visible and socially active.

Women in the West have long fought for reproductive and legal rights, with varying degrees of success. Theirs is a fight unfamiliar to Kurdish women. I know of people that had access to abortions in the 1980s. These people viewed abortion as a private matter, not a legal one, which is why they didn't bother to campaign for abortion rights. Consequently, abortion remains illegal, and expose women to illegal abortion clinics, or self-induced abortion, which can lead to death.

My mother and I agree that reproductive rights are central to the feminist effort, given that they call for personal sovereignty and autonomous choice. She told me that although it was socially accepted for married women to have abortions in Kurdistan, the story was quite different for single women. The latter had to undergo the procedure in total secrecy. The situation in Kurdistan has not changed for single women, because the need for an abortion is evidence of sexual activity — and it matters not whether said activity occurred freely or was coerced. When discovered to have had or sought an abortion, women in Kurdistan can become victims of honour. This deadly attitude has not changed, and given the social value of chastity — in its varying definitions — people have done little to fight for the reproductive rights of single women.

Women's rights activists and members of parliament only fight for women's rights in areas that are not publicly taboo. The right to live, freedom from violence are spoken about regularly, but beyond that, there exists little room to discuss the need for reform on Kurdish societal perceptions of what constitutes an "appropriate right" for women. How can rights be appropriated? If such rights are to exist, they must be fundamental, not conditional.

The patriarchal ideology of chastity requires unmarried women to remain celibate, while men explore boundless sexual activity with women. As things stand, respectable men may have sex with several women, but respectable women may not. This is because in patriarchal societies people view women as pure — not unlike the Virgin Mary. Such impositions are not placed on men, who in return, do as they please.

Women who depict themselves differently are

socially ostracised. Throughout the Kurdistan Region, hefty moral codes are imposed on women, and in essence such moral codes only retain meaning if they are applied to both men and women.

What's perhaps strange to many people, is that a woman wearing a headscarf would readily challenge conventional attitudes towards chastity, which are often at the expense of women's autonomy. Undoubtedly, throughout the past years many people have attempted to undermine both my religious affiliation and perception of feminism, simply because the patriarchal ideals they want to espouse are exposed.

It is crucial that we are not cornered into justifying how we dress because once we succumb to that platform where we are forced to provide an explanation, we inevitably substantiate other people's ability to question, interrogate and challenge our way of living.

The situation of Kurdish women in the Kurdistan Region is vastly different from other parts of the region because of the deep integration of patriarchy in both religion and politics. Men continue to dominate politics, and do little to promote women as their equals in the political sphere. This situation is not exclusive to Kurdistan region, of course; male-dominated politics remain a global problem. The significant difference, however, is that some parts of the world provide more opportunities for women to participate politically. Unfortunately, little is done to encourage young women to be politically active without being perceived as an opportunist, again, unlike male counterparts.

It is noteworthy to mention that during the emergence of Islamic State (IS) in Iraq in 2014, and Syria beforehand, Kurdish women played a key role in fighting the extremists from making territorial advances beyond Iraq's second largest city Mosul, and the autonomous Kurdish canton of Kobane, situated on the border of Syria and Turkey.

Women's suffering is not limited to the political landscape. Recent legislation against gender-based violence has not changed repressive attitudes towards women. It has only cleared the government of responsibility, given that officials can now claim the relative legislation have been passed to protect women from violence. It is not sufficient to pass laws that address violence against women without challenging the societal attitude towards them. The government should, in fact must, support local organisations that ensure women understand how the law protects them, and how they can act upon it, and begin to incorporate them in the cultural milieu.

To me, feminism in Kurdistan Region has yet to emerge. Women shy away from labelling themselves as such, in fear of being branded as different. In 2012, the creation of a feminist society in Erbil attracted few people, among them my partner. It was not shocking to me that only a handful of people turned up for the meeting but it was upsetting that no one among them wanted to take it further.

A feminist revolution in the region entails changing the societal perception of women in all spheres, and demanding an end to institutions that directly discriminate against women. This does not end with passing a few preliminary laws that allow women to hold men legally liable when their rights are violated in cases of domestic violence, but it challenges the region on all sectors — business, politics, education, health and so on.

The fact that the majority of companies are headed by men, and there is only one female minister, is sufficient to highlight the dire situation of women in the Kurdistan Region's fight for equality. Challenging honour notions alone is not sufficient in eradicating patriarchal establishments, instead young people — men and women alike — must work together towards equality.

BEAUTY

"A cultural fixation on female thinness is not an obsession about female beauty but an obsession about female obedience."

Naomi Wolf

Whitening products are widely available throughout the Kurdistan Region. Slimming products, the miraculous pomegranate pill, the herbal tea that magically makes you shed pounds, and appetite control pills are a booming industry. Women are increasingly fixated on their weight throughout the world, the goal to attain that level of appropriate thinness to be loved, accepted, cherished, idolised, and desired, is worldwide.

It's not just a skeleton-thin image that people are

obsessed with, but instead a spandex-modelled thin body, with a small bust and huge, almost gigantic Kim Kardashian backside. It is curves cultivated in places that no one had thought of a few centuries ago for the purposes of our bodies conforming to a notion of sex appeal.

Two centuries prior in the Kurdistan Region, desirable women were curvaceous and had modest bosoms. The beauty ideal has changed but it continues to devalue women because it measures worth according to appearance, a fabricated concept.

The false beauty myth forced upon women causes self-hatred, particularly in adolescents and young women. Sooner or later they begin to detest their nose, weight, lips, teeth, bones, legs, cheeks....you get the point. They begin to believe that their lives and features will improve if they lose weight. They imagine more friends and admirers, higher grades, more respect and popularity. The illusion continues until women approach menopause (or earlier) and turn desperately to surgery in hopes of maintaining or recreating youth. At that point the chance to grow old gracefully goes under the knife, quite literally.

In 2008, while visiting a small province in the Kurdistan Region, I stayed with a family whose young daughters had blonde hair, hazel eyes and beautiful tanned skin. The first time we spoke, the children complimented my "lighter" skin. It was raining, and the girls placed buckets in their garden to capture water falling from the skies. Their simplicity, odd ways, wit and lightheartedness were captivating. So I stood outside as the rain poured down. The fresh smell of the soil filled the air, and the trees shone as raindrops washed dirt from their leaves.

The next morning the girls washed their faces with the water in the buckets. They laughed and started a water fight. They explained that the rain would lighten their skin because of the particular month in which it had fallen. It was strange for me to hear this because in London I was raised in a social context that prized tanned skin. As a teenager I spent hours in parks with friends at the first sight of the rare London sunshine. We would rub Vaseline on our faces and hands hoping that our skin would absorb sunlight and become tanned. I told the girls that there were people in London who desired their complexion and spent money buying products to darken their skin. The girls looked puzzled. They could not understand why anyone would wish for darker skin. I hope one day they will learn to appreciate their skin tone without associating beauty with white or black.

Beauty is a tool of patriarchy. People base contemporary depictions of women on the notion of a feminine ideal that does not exist in reality. Kurdish women have yet to publicly challenge the beauty ideals that constantly pressure them to alter their bodies. But their lack of criticism does not reflect support for current beauty fashions; it simply shows that a cultural revolution is further on the horizon.

Perhaps people are not yet ready for a feminist revolution in Kurdistan. Women are not angry enough to launch a coordinated uprising against patriarchy. But the time will come and then women will protest against the media and the tormenting images used to portray them. Women will no longer accept repressive feminine norms, such as the idolised virgin turned goddess. They will compel the government to include women in politics and ensure that they are not merely a voiceless quota to fill government seats for a better international image.

CONFLICTING IDENTITIES

"Appreciation for cultural diversity is essential for our co-existence."

Lailah Gifty Akita

I have met many young women of the Kurdish diaspora who find themselves locked within conflicted realities between Western ideals and their families' cultural practices. Some families do not understand that even if the Kurdish youth maintains some aspects of Kurdish culture in the West, they still become assimilated in a social system different from Kurdish culture and religions. Some of these young people fear sharing their views with family members, and rarely challenge the aspects of Kurdish culture at odds with those of their new host country. This conflict often creates a double life for diaspora youth, some of whom pretend to support certain Kurdish values, while they live as free, unrestricted, autonomous beings in Western societies.

The different perceptions of identities should be understood as a natural occurrence. When you live somewhere for a prolonged time, undoubtedly, that place will shape or even change your mindset for better or worse. The problem is, families that retain a rigid perception of appropriated behaviour within Kurdish families in the West tend to face difficulties, pushing their children away in the process.

Take Lillian for instance, a 19-year-old biomedicine student, unsure of where her studies will take her in the future. She entered the field because her parents wanted her to explore an area related to medicine, despite her wish to concentrate on the humanities. It was difficult for Lillian to challenge her parents, particularly after a university offered her entry to its biomedical program. Consequently, Lillian moved forward with plans that pleased her parents, succumbing to their pressure.

Lillian lived in London. Her parents did not allow her to rent a room on the university campus, or share one off-campus with another student because they felt it inappropriate for a Kurdish girl to have such freedoms without parental guidance. Lillian said she wished to live on campus, but her parents would not allow it because they felt it contradicted Kurdish values (values which she herself did not hold). Her parents thus prevented Lillian from sharing housing with other students, so she had to take a long train journey to attend classes.

Lillian introduced me to Gelawej, who I also interviewed to gain a diverse perspective on the lives and experiences of Kurdish girls. Gelawej's parents had allowed her to move from Manchester to London, where she could live on her university campus. (The distance between the two cities is about 196 miles.) During the application process, Gelawej had applied to several universities outside of Manchester so she could ensure more freedom. She said: "I hated the restrictions my parents imposed on me when I was a teenager. They never tried to understand me or how I thought; they just assumed I agreed with everything they said, which I didn't."

Gelawej looked comfortable wearing a short dress, attire which some Kurdish families would find too explicit or revealing. She had an answer for this: "How I dress is my business. My clothes don't diminish my modesty. This is my life, and those who try to judge me, judge only themselves."

Gelawej was not the only one who seemed tired of parental control. Many of the Kurdish girls I met and interviewed in London shared similar concerns. One of them, Shereen, said she got a tattoo when she was 17, a fact she had concealed from her family. She loved tattoos and planned to get more after she married. Shereen told me she kept only a few Kurdish friends on her social networks because she found most Kurds to be "gossip-crazed people far more concerned with people's clothing on Facebook pictures than with their own lives." Shereen, a student activist, shared a house with several people. She said her perspective on life was incompatible with Kurdish culture because the latter was fixated on women. She left me with this thought: "No one questions what the sons and daughters of Kurdish officials do in the West; like their drinking sprees and night-club partying, which some Kurdish people would find offensive. But when average young Kurds do the same, suddenly there's an explosion of moral panic."

Shanar is a law student living with her parents. She is not particularly fond of studying law, but found it more bearable than medicine. Shanar perceives little purpose in attending university, since she works as a retail managing assistant and believes her high school education is enough to give her a solid beginning in the industry. Lillian, Gelawej, Shereen and Shanar have something in common: All three women felt disengaged from Kurdish culture, which they understood their parents valued, but created conflict for the younger generation. Although this sense of disconnection has distanced some Kurds raised abroad, it has also inspired others to campaign for the rights of Kurdish people and promote social awareness about their plight. Like any other people, the Kurds have diverse views on politics and religion. Many of them are finding ways to exercise autonomy without vitiating their choice of lifestyle.

Some Kurdish parents tend to envision a life for their children that is similar to the one they wished for themselves. Like most parents, they want what is best for their children, even if the best requires sending them in a direction they oppose. What I find problematic is when parents refuse to accept that adolescents become young adults and form their own perspective about life. This inability to respect their children's opinions — when they are no longer children — is unhealthy because human beings are different; we cannot expect everyone to have the same views and live life in the same way.

The above examples can not be used to generalise about Kurdish parents in the West. There are many freedom-championing parents that allow their children, particularly daughters to pursue their ambitions with little restriction, but it definitely highlights a growing divide between those from traditionally conservative parents and those who are more liberal.

PRESERVING KURDISH CULTURE

"My heritage has been my grounding, and it has brought me peace."

Maureen O'Hara

I had to be careful when I interviewed people in Kurdistan, mainly because some questions that seem appropriate in English can be offensive in Kurdish. I worked hard to present myself as a cultured person. My interviews consumed all my time, leaving none to visit relatives. When I finally squeezed in some time to visit a maternal great aunt, it was long overdue and somewhat awkward, given my prolonged absence from the region. But she welcomed me into her home and hugged me for some time. I hugged her tightly in return, and it felt like I had known her my whole life. The visit was refreshing; aunt Kafiya is a marvellous keeper of history.

There is a rise in nationalism in Kurdistan. This is mainly because people want to salvage their culture, particularly since Kurdish history is mostly undocumented and people have struggled to preserve their heritage amid wars and genocide. The little we know, we rarely discuss, which is dangerous given that the older generations will not live forever, and when their time comes they will take the stories that give cultural identity to the Kurdish people. There is, thankfully, one solution to this problem: Codification. The best way to preserve Kurdish history and cultural identity is by creating written records that respect historical events remembered by Kurds. Thus far, the absence of this method has caused significant confusion and only scattered scraps of information about the various Kurdish territories, which we call Kurdistan are available through first-hand testimony.

Even in a increasingly globalised world, where technology helps people create a unified culture, it remains important to preserve knowledge and customs established by various ethnic groups. As Kurds we have left behind some practices that enrich our human experience. For example, whereas before all Kurdish children could play on the streets of Erbil, today contemporary society makes it increasingly harder for girls.

As a young child I lived in Erbil with my family, while my father worked in Darbandikhan, a province on the outskirts of Slemani. During that time he travelled back and forth to work, until disagreement between political parties left them on the brink of civil war. The conflict, of course, was partly sparked by the brutal policies of Saddam Saddam, who hindered progress in the region for years, as the world would come to know. It was during that time, when the political situation worsened, that the entire family moved to Darbandikhan, from which I treasure most of my childhood memories. My mother, on the other hand, never quite adjusted to life in Darbandikhan, as is often the case for adults whose relocation leaves friends behind.

In my neighbourhood the girls played together and the boys on their own. Although parents did not allow boys and girls to play together all the time, all children could enjoy time outdoors. In the afternoons our parents gave us small change and we ran to the local shops to buy Kurdish chewing gum, sunflower seeds and sweets. Usually each child received one dinar, so we had to combine our resources to buy all the goodies we wanted — which we did and shared in great fun. I remember fondly one warm summer afternoon when we bought two watermelons and received a free one along with the usual seeds and sweets (and we considered this to be quite adventurous).

My family home was the nearest to the shops, so after hours playing outside we usually sat in our garden resting like royalty. There I picked and washed cucumbers, sprinkled them with salt and ate them with my friends. We savoured them, as we discussed our dreams. Sometimes we played with Barbie dolls, other times we turned them into little monsters. In retrospect it seems sadistic, but in childhood it was merely good, innocent fun. Many of my young friends could sew. They sat sewing tiny dresses and pajamas for their dolls. I was not allowed to play with needles, so I watched them, marvelling at how quickly their little fingers moved through the fabric.

In late afternoons I often begged my mother for permission to ride my bike to a nearby neighbourhood, where my best friend Kajal lived. We had become friends when her mother was a domestic worker for my family, and remained close until I left Kurdistan. I loved Kajal dearly, but sadly more than 16 years have passed since we last met, despite my numerous attempts to find her during yearly visits.

After hours of begging, my mother would finally consent and I would mount my bike and ride as fast as I could to see Kajal. Many times I stopped along the way to visit other friends, whose mothers thought they were sleeping until their enthusiastic heads appeared at windows. They would soon join me outside for a game of Mooriyanni, which consisted of children throwing jewels and beads into a hole from a distance. As a frequent cheater, I would often win and leave my friends crying for the loss of precious items.

Kajal was adventurous, creative and strong. She taught me to make beaded necklaces and headbands. She was fearless and we often played together, eventually becoming best friends, but that friendship has never been rekindled. I don't know where she lives, whether she is married or even alive.

During Eid al-Fitr, a festival that celebrates the end of Ramadan, my mother would dress me in fancy clothing and adorn me with a gold necklace and matching earrings. She would brush my hair back under colourful headbands or hold it with butterfly shaped clips covered with small gems. The ritual made me feel special. Once ready I would take a bag and ride my bicycle to Kajal's house. There we would greet each other with an enthusiastic "Merry Eid!" and run outside to knock on every neighbourhood door, asking for sweets, as was customary for children during Eid holidays. The neighbours were quite generous and usually filled our bags with enough candy to last several weeks. Kajal and I would split our goods evenly, so that we both had a taste of everything. I am so grateful for my childhood in Kurdistan. It enriched my life and gave me a solid grounding of Kurdish culture. I grew up feeling equal to everyone and this is the fundamental value that guides my decisions. I recognise that my personal philosophies derive in great part from the decision my parents made to encourage their children to appreciate people from all walks of life.

Today Kurdish children no longer play on the streets. They have not learned traditional games an many do not visit neighbours during Eid, as done in the old days. Many girls do not dare to ride bicycles and circle neighbourhoods like curious cats. People have changed the way they raise children, who now begin to worry about appearance much too early and consider romantic relationships even before adolescence. Years ago we nurtured Kurdish culture far more than we do now. It would be easy to blame globalisation for our disconnect with the past, but it is not progress that distances us from culture; it is a lack of interest.

MARRIAGE AND FREEDOM

"The thing women have yet to learn is nobody gives you power. You just take it."

Roseanne Barr

My aunt Hilda habitually visits the elderly home in Erbil. She buys modest gifts for the residents and sometimes offers them home-cooked food. She is middle aged, but never married, which is odd for a Kurdish woman. Interestingly, she remains single not by choice, but by circumstance. When she was young, her family had rather high standards and demanded only perfection in potential suitors. This excluded most men available.

Tired of the hassle involved in assessing

suitors, Hilda resisted the idea of marriage, and the years only increased her standards, diminishing her chances to find the perfect husband.

Marriage in Kurdistan can at times become an institution of patriarchy that does not stand on equal footing for men and women. Responsibilities involving the arrangement of marriage fall on the shoulders of men, instead of being evenly distributed between future spouses. This social custom cements men in the role of sole providers and women in that of mere receivers. It is a process that excludes women from financial decisions concerning the wedding and house preparations. For the wedding, custom demands women to wear intricate gold jewellery and other luxurious items — all provided by the groom, which he does readily to ensure no one questions his character. These practices set the tone of burden for men and dependency for women, marking their union early on with imbalance.

There is no reason why material and control should sustain marriage, rather than love, respect, friendship, trust and honesty. Kurdish culture has infused marriage with inflexible values that force a private relationship into the focal lens of society.

New wives are falsely convinced that within two years of marriage they must have a baby to ground their husbands in the home and keep them from looking elsewhere. Hanar, a 25-year-old part-time pharmacist in Slemani, has one daughter. Like many other women she believes this. "Every marriage needs a child to survive. A home without children is empty, it gives the husband nothing to go home to. People start talking if you don't have children." I was alarmed to hear an educated woman give voice to these expectations of married women, particularly because I believe people (not relatives) should be able to decide when to have children.

Hanar found me naive. "You will soon understand, you're young now, but you'll see things differently when you're married." When I look back on this interview, I noted that I hoped marriage will never change my ideas of equality and cooperation between men and women. In fact, believing in anything opposite would be a sign that patriarchy had overtaken my sensibilities. At any rate, I have observed that while many single people look forward to marriage, some of those who are married often yearn for its end.

The evening Hanar and I chatted was warm and crispy. We stood in front of her house enjoying a breathtaking view of Slemani. My stomach was heavy from the local delicacies we had consumed at dinner. When I left Hanar, I hoped to meet other young women who held more diverse views of marriage. I did not want to depart the beautiful city without meeting feminists willing to challenge the common misunderstandings of Kurdish culture, as applied in contemporary society. I was scheduled to leave the area early the next morning, but remained late in the province to interview young women about gender discrimination. During this period in Slemani, I knew few activists and people.

The roads to Erbil, unlike what I remember from childhood, were free from unnecessary checkpoints and sectarian flags. I recall only one checkpoint, where a kind policemen checked our documents and wished us well on our journey. The early morning air was thin, marked by a cold breeze. I had packed peanut butter and jelly sandwiches for the journey (I kid!), as my stomach had yet to adjust to local food from the restaurants along the way to Erbil. It had been difficult, however, to resist eating the yoghurt with tea and naan bread.

When we reached Erbil, my native city and where my parents were raised, I was eager to walk around town. After a quick stop at my grandmother's house, I went to the small home my parents had bought to accommodate our family during visits. It is located in an area where mostly local Kurds live, which is advantageous, as it allows me to mingle with them, participate in their lives, and welcome them into mine. I was not one born to live in mansions or ivory towers detached from the realities of society. I appreciate being in the heart of a vibrant community of working people.

That evening I resumed work. While translating and transcribing my interviews with local people, I came to the recording of a conversation with Bella, a law student from the Slemani area, home to my brother-in-law's mother. Bella had beautiful tanned skin, long curly hair and large brown eyes that deepened when she emphasised a point. Her gentle demeanour supported a smart, articulate style that showed femininity and strength could be in harmony. When she spoke of marriage and patriarchy in an assertive, unapologetic tone, her words reverberated like music to my ears. Brave and ready for change, Bella symbolised the soul of Kurdish feminism, and I hoped to see her become a leader in Kurdistan. Her story was moving; she had lost her father, a Peshmerga, to guerrilla warfare early in life. Instead of remarrying as did most widows, her mother had raised the couple's four children on the income she earned as a seamstress of traditional Kurdish dresses. As they became older, Bella's siblings had worked weekends at fruit markets to help the family. Bella describes her mother as a proud, iron lady — the Margaret Thatcher in the house.

The experience of dignified survival taught Bella that women can only change Kurdish society by example. She says, "Women talk about change and the elements of discrimination in societies, but they fail to exact the change they want."

Women are raised to believe that their will and determination come from husbands, and that marriage thus offers independence. "Is there anything more damaging and humiliating than this?" Bella asks sharply. She continues: "We are not mules. We are humans of equal worth and ability. Our weaknesses are human. When we criticise society and reject oppression, we will be liberated! When we regain control of our bodies and make decisions without seeking permission, we will be free!" Bella's voice had fire, to which no English translation can do justice.

When I finished working on Bella's interview, it was time for dinner, and my aunts were in the house making tea and warming food prepared earlier. They chatted happily, as they moved about the kitchen and dining room. I sat watching them, still moved by Bella's words, which reminded me that I was not alone in my expectations for Kurdish women.

Epiphany struck and I decided then to find more women like Bella and me. Until that moment I had spent so much time meeting women who had been physically or psychologically battered, that I had forgotten to focus on the women who rise above abuse to challenge patriarchy in thought and action.

One cannot classify Kurdish women into only

two categories. There are several, all of which reveal multiple experiences and family traditions that shape unique personalities. However, for my research, I found it important to discern between the women who had been systematically victimised and those who had not. This required an elementary definition of victim, which I assigned in context: Kurdish victims lived in patriarchal households and adhered to repressive honour values they could not defy because of social pressure and financial dependency; non-victims lived free from from both physical and psychological oppression, as exemplified by Bella and her mother. Nonetheless, the distinction between female victim and non-victim does not represent the circumstances of all Kurdish women. It simply guides my investigation of Kurdish feminism. Clearly there is a large grey area, and we cannot lump all Kurdish women within a basic concept of extremes. Such an approach would be narrow and neglectful.

ARRANGED MARRIAGES

"My first marriage was an arranged marriage. I arranged it myself."

Jarod Kintz

Arranged marriages used to be an important part of Kurdish culture, but are less common now that men and women interact more and are less keen about entering marriage 'blind'. In the West many people do not understand that there is a difference between forced and arranged marriages. Kurds usually find their future spouses at universities and through participation in social events. They do not date in a western sense, but tradition demands that men, not women, express interest in starting a relationship. Such a first move varies according to individual style, and can include a man asking a woman for her telephone number, inquiring if she is interested in marriage, or asking her parents for her hand in marriage before he even speaks with her.

Nevertheless, when it comes to pairing, men are consistently the ones who first approach women, which puts them in a disadvantaged position. While socially it is not acceptable for women to make the first move and demonstrate interest in men, the latter must do precisely that. This cultural tradition prevents women from choosing a partner in the first round of considerations, so invariably they marry a man from a pool of candidates they did not select. From what I can see, there is more convenience than logic in this old partnering system, of which, Asiya, an 18-year-old student, said: "It would be odd for a girl to choose a man, and the girl would sell herself cheap." Note the words she chose in reference to women. Why would the conscious choice of romance make a girl "sell herself cheap"? If anything, I would think that such attitude shows autonomy. Do men sell themselves cheap when they approach women and propose marriage? Do men lose worth when they make the first move and accept vulnerability? I think we should scrutinise the faulty logic in a system that bends rules unfavourably toward one gender.

My sister had an arranged marriage. The man who is now her husband contacted our family to show his interest in her after they had met at a Kurdish conference in London. With our parents' knowledge, my sister and her suitor had a casual date to acquaint themselves a bit more, before deciding to marry, which they did based on the little they had learned of each other. The two are highly educated and worldly, so their choice to marry did not surprise us, given their compatibility and common interests. It also helped that my father was quite fond of the groom.

My sister's father-in-law was also a cultivated man, fiercely committed to social advancement. He had taught children in Kurdistan when teachers already subsisted on a meagre income. In the 1960s he received an offer to study at Oxford University, an opportunity he missed owing to family circumstances. This only encouraged him to promote a legacy of education, which he provided to many students, who still speak fondly of him. It was his reputation that won my brother-in-law an esteemed position in my father's heart in the early stages of the courtship.

My sister is not the only woman in our family who had an arranged marriage; our mother did too. In the 1940s my father had been searching for a wife, but had not found the right person until he saw our mother. He describes their first encounter: "When I first saw her, her eyes looked green. She was slender and dazzling. Later I discovered much to my surprise that her eyes were not green. This did not matter; she had already stolen my heart." They were soon engaged and married. But first they defied their conservative community and went to the movie theatre in Erbil. The adventure was more eventful than they had anticipated, as my grandfather found them and later drove them home. Some considered it inappropriate for unmarried couples to attend the cinema together, even if engaged in the 1940s. This was mainly so that if they canceled plans to marry no one would have reason to speak of them unfavourably — the sort of gossip Kurdish people still fear and enjoy.

Arranged marriages can help people conveniently find a partner, especially in Kurdish societies, but in a fair world men and women should have equal lead in the process. There is nothing shameful in showing interest in someone, or for a father to find his daughter suitable partners. Waiting for the knight in shining armour to arrive will turn the hairs of many grey before they realise that this mythical ideal exists mostly to keep women powerless and incapable of making decisions.

Although ultimately most Kurdish women can decide whether or not to marry a man, people should respect their power of choice in all stages — from selecting potential suitors for consideration to consenting. Much to the contrary of what many believe, religion itself does not forbid women from making solid choices. In fact, in the case of Islam, there is a precedent that allows and encourages women to actively choose a spouse. How have so many Kurdish Muslims overlooked this pressing detail? To be free, women must have autonomy in all aspects of their life. They must make decisions, and men and women ought to respect this important component of a truly honourable life.

It is not easy to challenge social expectations,

even when they violate women's basic freedoms. Moreover, as demonstrated earlier, women sometimes propagate unjust beliefs that hurt their cause for an equal standing in society. As women, we can be our own worst enemies when we defend supposed religious and cultural practices that curtail our freedom; and seldom do we stand together against the tyrannical institutions that oppress our gender. Patriarchy finds a foundation in all institutions that concern women, including marriage, which is one of the most sacred of Kurdish society. Although marriage as such is clearly a patriarchal tool, many rush to it only to learn that the liberty they had expected from marriage does not exist. In my interviews with newlyweds, I have heard some dispute this interpretation and others concur. However, I noticed that many feel embarrassed discussing the topic and thus reveal only a fraction of their problems; while others enjoy a healthy marriage, and prefer not to blame patriarchy for minor problems.

ACTIVISM IN TURMOIL

"How wonderful it is that nobody need wait a single moment before starting to improve the world."

Anne Frank

At some point in life, many people become passionate about philanthropic causes and make a concentrated effort to promote them. This may include undertaking activities that support human and animals rights, child welfare, the arts or political participation. We all have unique convictions, but some of us take our convictions a step further. We believe we can enforce change through effective campaigning, so we spend our time fighting, arguing and protesting to ensure it happens. In doing so, we often neglect other aspects of our lives. Some neglect having or being in a relationship, others give their appearance little concern, or family little attention.

My colleagues and I have sacrificed different parts of our lives. Some of us have avoided relationships and marriage to prioritise our activism without having to neglect the people we love; others have sacrificed attention to their families and given little importance to social gatherings. It is difficult, if not impossible, to strike a perfect balance between activism and personal life. In my case, social life has taken a back seat to campaign priorities.

I joined the Alliance for Kurdish Rights in 2009 which has grown steadily since under new editorial guidelines that have shifted the neutrality of its political stance on various issues. In the beginning we had few sponsors, so the funds covered only the costs of website maintenance and security. We blogged voluntarily with the help of various journalists who shared information, and we used social media to connect with Kurds scattered throughout the globe. Always receptive to our cause, I often received communications from people dispatching human rights news, as I walked to work or classes at my university. Dedicated activism is for sure a round the clock job.

We remained vigilant for relevant news so that we could effectively mobilise people for protests, amass petitions and prepare activists to lobby. Since Kurdish people live throughout the world, it takes time to organise action. For example, when an earthquake struck in Van, an extremely poor area of Turkey populated by Kurdish people, the local government was slow to respond, so Kurds everywhere raised funds to help. Our organisation helped raise awareness about the event, and tried to support local charities that helped people in the aftermath of the disaster.

One of the most difficult aspects of being a Kurdish activist involves undergoing subtle personality changes. For me, this is the case because I do not support ideals that people have used as control methods against women. This has made me necessarily stern to survive in my work. The lessons have been learned the hard way; when I was kind and lenient with other organisations, they often disregarded Kurdish issues with little consideration. It became clear that a more detached approach was necessary to yield positive results. This entailed having to negotiate cautiously and being aware of peoples' motives. I have learned that to effect change, female activists must discard the patriarchal feminine ideals usually projected on young women. This demands being more aggressive in arguments, which makes the older generation of Kurds rather uncomfortable. They do not like it and are not accustomed to being challenged by younger people. I was raised to be open-minded and outspoken. It is not my problem (or my family's) that other people feel offended when I respectfully challenge their views. Civilised dialogue based on reason must not bend for gender. I am foremost a human being, a thinker, and I cherish my existence as a woman in this wide context.

Kurdish people at conferences and concerned relatives often advise me to "enjoy life." They seem to perceive my activism at the time as something that prevents happiness. I feel offended when people insist that I could use a long holiday, or say that online activism is useless. I cannot enforce change on a governmental level, but there are thousands like me who effectively promote Kurdish rights, and try to inspire change at the top. Digital activists do enjoy life, and in fact develop a keen appreciation for it, given their understanding of freedom, which they feel privileged to enjoy. I know of activists less privileged, who have been imprisoned, assaulted, tortured and killed in their struggle for human rights. As people regularly exposed to stories of injustice, we especially value life. I am not certain that I can say the same of people who urge relaxation for those concerned with humanity.

The number of Kurdish activists is growing consistently, but unfortunately it includes opportunists — people more interested in publicising their name than advancing Kurdish rights. Such are usually the first to speak and last to volunteer in places that need help. When we hosted events they were not present to arrange tables and prepare food because they perceived these tasks as insignificant, when in fact these details are essential at conferences and events.

Logistical and political divisions among Kurdish activists have created several organisations supported by various groups, some politically motivated, others not. The Alliance for Kurdish Rights began with the goal to avoid politics and promote Kurdish rights globally. The central idea was to give a voice to vulnerable Kurds. It is unfortunate that Europe's numerous Kurdish organisations either lack unity or withhold support from Alliance for Kurdish Rights organisation because of its reluctance to become a vessel for political agendas. Although, the organisation since my departure has changed dramatically, it is nonetheless a valuable front to highlight Kurdish issues that are often neglected by mainstream media outlets.

The lack of unity among activists and Kurdish organisations disrupts effectiveness and hinders progress. When all entities vocalise outrage about similar issues at different times, and protest on different dates, they squander collaboration and scatter any potential for a true Kurdish alliance. Moreover, this fragmentation does not bode well for public relations. Kurdish people need to unite globally on common ground to be effective. Only in this manner can we increase visibility and strengthen our voice.

I left Alliance for Kurdish Rights in 2012, and since leaving I have worked with various organisations, but during that period of blogging on Kurdish Rights, I became aware of the countless struggles we have as a nation, and the need for an organisation to emerge, highlighting the plight of Kurdish people without limitations of funding or political party agenda.

SOCIAL MEDIA AND KURDISH RIGHTS

"Social media is the ultimate equaliser. It gives a voice and a platform to anyone willing to engage."

Amy Jo Martin.

Kurdish activists have been using social media consistently and collectively, even more so since the Arab Spring, to campaign for different causes. The revolutions that took place in the Arab world in 2011 confirmed for activists that they could use social media to create online campaigns and raise awareness to engineer change in Middle East. Although it would be inaccurate to credit Twitter and Facebook entirely for the success of the Arab revolutions in ousting dictatorships, we must recognise their essential role in mobilising people and international support, particularly as the rebellion in Tahrir Square progressed and government agents began to attack protesters. When mainstream news outlets missed the early stages of the Arab uprising, citizen journalists turned to Twitter, reporting in huge volume around the clock. It was then that established news channels like CNN and the BBC began to report on the revolts that had followed a fruit vendor's desperate act to protest abuse from officials in Tunisia. Activists of the Kurdish struggle are now following suit, and in places like Turkey, where there is media censorship, Kurds have increasingly turned to social media to inform, remain informed and effectively campaign for Kurdish rights.

In the past Turkey censored the Kurdish press, and unidentified attackers targeted Kurdish journalists. At times newspapers were forced to close following the killing, battery or imprisonment of staff members. Attackers often burned newsstands selling Kurdish papers and attacked newsagents. For instance in 1992, a Kurdish newspaper — Özgür Gündem — closed temporarily after criminals murdered four of its journalists. In

1994, the bombing of Özgür Ülke newspaper killed one staff member and injured 23 others. Yahya Orhan, Huseyin Deniz and Hafiz Akdemir are some of the journalists lost in the general violence directed at the Kurdish press. Today the situation is less deadly for Kurds because people do not always follow mainstream and print media. The internet now allows people to access and disseminate information instantly, globally, and network with others to mobilise hundreds overnight to protest against criminal injustice. In the past the Kurdish press suffered more at great human cost because abuses were contained locally, in secrecy. Now with digital and social media the world is watching, and this increases safety for persecuted groups like the Kurds.

Safety is not always guaranteed and is still far from certain. Violence against Kurdish people remains a serious problem, as evidenced in Uludere when Turkish warplanes bombed Kurdish civilians crossing the border from Iraq in late 2011. Most of the 35 killed were teenagers. The Turkish military may have been targeting members of the Kurdistan Workers' Party (PKK), but no excuse justifies slaughtering innocent people. I remember hearing the news that day in the early hours of morning, when various people reported via Twitter that a village had been attacked. In the UK we did not know which village, so we continued to communicate, terribly concerned for what may have happened. Within hours, the tragedy became clearer, as people reached activists in Turkey and its areas heavily populated with Kurdish people. From afar we learned that there had been a night raid in Uludere, in the province of Sirnak, where residents were without electricity and roads were blocked because of heavy snow. People reported seeing bodies scattered in the region, completely unrecognisable, making it very difficult for locals to identify the dead and notify families.

Many Kurdish activists would not sleep that day. We lacked precise information of what had taken place and this was extremely disconcerting. Nonetheless we added a brief update on the Alliance for Kurdish Rights website, mentioning we had been in contact with activists in Turkey. In light of the uncertainty, we deliberately withheld their names to safeguard their identity. By later morning we received the heartbreaking details of the massacre at Uludere. The victims had been teenage boys carrying diesel fuel from Iraq to sell in their village. They were all under 21, one of them just 12 years old. The information became clearer when we received pictures, which spread like wildfire on Facebook and Twitter. Soon young British Kurds walked to Kings Cross Station in central London and stopped traffic. They carried flags, placards and chanted slogans. Police arrested some of them to clear the roads, but in less than 24 hours global activists joined the fight for Kurdish rights and the next day thousands protested in several countries despite the very short notice.

Protesters amassed in several European cities and some American states. Most Kurdish regions held protests and vigils. During their funeral procession, thousands surrounded the young victims' coffins, which Kurds carried on their shoulders. The Alliance for Kurdish Rights received photographs of the event, as those present continued to tweet from protests and the procession. Many were sad, angry, disheartened, frustrated, but the tragedy taught Kurdish activists something new.

Young people's unity and condemnation of the Uludere atrocity inspired Kurdish activists and gave them a stronger sense of purpose. We began to believe that with organised defiance we could achieve goals. We learned that in collaboration there is immeasurable power, and this facilitates efficient responses to catastrophe. We came to understand that collective work is more fruitful than individual activism. Although we felt unsatisfied with the Turkish response to the Uludere disaster, we remained motivated to continue our work for justice, particularly as the prime minister of Turkey admitted faulty intelligence had caused the killings and offered condolences to the families but no formal apology. It was also heartening to see the Peace and Democratic Party of Turkey gather in the country's parliament to protest against brutality towards Kurdish people.

Despite the Turkish government's recognition of the serious blunder at Uludere, Kurdish people felt that more was in order. As history shows, this was not the first time Turkish warplanes had attacked Kurdish villagers. In August 2011 an air strike in northern Southern Kurdistan had killed seven members of one Kurdish family, but authorities denied responsibility before launching a proper investigation or addressing grievances.

Servet Encu, 31, was the sole survivor and oldest of the Uludere massacre, but Turkish newspapers did not interview him to share his astonishing story of survival. Although some Turkish officials paid respects to the family of one victim, none visited or called Servet and the other families to offer support. The country seemed to deliberately forget him and disregard the bloodbath he had endured. People shoved him aside as an irrelevant topic, with no regard for his thoughts or sorrow over having witnessed the horrific death of his young friends. The national neglect and blatant dis- respect for human life widened the gap and slammed the doors of communication between the Turkish government and Kurdish people.

The year 2013 marked our greatest effort so far to encourage people to use social media. A smartphone with enough credit to access the internet can facilitate activism. It also helps people locate and submit information to journalists worldwide. In areas like Uludere, the use of social media is vital. When a village suffers air strikes, local people need to have the means to report them; when young activists are apprehended, their families and friends must be able to inform the media immediately, to prevent brutality. Those of us in safe cities can publicise this information, gain support for their release and pressure governments to honour justice and pay reparations. With the help of social media we can do all this from afar without fearing for our lives.

Social media works like a loudspeaker; if you shout in a deserted area, no one will hear you, but if you shout in the presence of several people, there is a high chance that your words will influence at least one. For example, in January 2012 someone wrote on Twitter that several young people in Sirnak had fled to the mountains to avoid arrest. The author of the tweet reported that security forces were raiding the homes of people noted on a list they had drawn up. Within minutes of reading the tweet, we were able to contact people in Sirnak and confirm the incident.

Twitter is a valuable social medium because it can inform people and save lives. Paradoxically, it can also endanger lives when users reveal the location of activists in regions marked by deadly oppression. Twitter also offers challenges, since we cannot readily identify the legitimacy of reports. How do we discern between honest and dishonest reporters? How do we differentiate between accurate and inaccurate tweets? We have a system for this, it may not be perfect, but it has thus far proved reliable: We confirm an incident only after gathering the same information from 10 to 15 individuals. In the rare cases when only one person reports that activists or civilians have been seized, we try to locate contacts in the vicinity to confirm the information. This practice has also helped us build a global network of activists.

When I cannot confirm an event from London, where I live, I send a text message to local activists who have more resources to locate ground contacts in areas of turmoil. Through this manner of network, we try to reach victims and motivate the governments of oppressive regions to seek and hold perpetrators accountable for their crimes. Digital media allows us to publicly express outrage over specific injustices, and demotivate corrupt authorities from arresting or persecuting innocent people.

LEYLA

"I said to myself, you must be brave. You must not be afraid of anyone. You are only trying to get an education. You are not committing a crime."

Malala Yousafzai

In the spring of 2009, my mother and I visited a girl named Leyla, whose parents had removed her from secondary school. She was born in Shaqlawa, a town in the northeast of Erbil Province, but now lived in the city of Erbil with her parents. Their home was located in the central part of the city, but they were extremely poor. When we stood in front of their house I noticed faded blue paint and cracks on the concrete. The house was spacious with an open structure that formed one bedroom and one living room, which encompassed the dining area.

The kitchen was extremely small, and filled with piles of plates around a bright, unused sink. The floor was covered with an old rug. The family had a refrigerator in the alcove under a staircase leading to the roof, but it functioned only when struck on its right side. Once, as I walked toward the bathroom, I looked inside to find only empty space filled with putrid water. I kept silent and returned to the living area with a smile. This family had shown us hospitality, kindness, respect and friendship, so our decision to stay with them — despite the crushing poverty came easily. Through this experience I saw a less popular side of Kurdistan, and I experienced the deprivation that many poor people endure daily, but I learned a great deal about the resilience of people and how together we can work to improve conditions for everyone.

During our time with the family, my mother covered the financial costs of living so that we could eat satisfactorily and according to our customs. She provided all the luxuries we were accustomed to having, so the physical environment did not deprive us of familiar comforts. Our stay was temporary so that I could complete my research in that specific area, but it was long enough to paint an image of the difficulties Leyla's family endured. For example, Leyla was responsible for cleaning the house, so everyday she awoke early to wash dishes outside, instead of using the defunct kitchen sink. She set the dining table with boiled eggs, fried eggs, cheese and eggs fried together, solid cheese, yoghurt, yogurt fat, olives, boiled peas and myriad seasoning containers. My London morning routine, which consists of absorbing news from my laptop, eating french toast and drinking tea, paled in comparison. Our lives differed significantly, but I understood that although I enjoyed more privileges and modern luxuries, Leyla was more optimistic.

When I asked Leyla about her plans for the future, she revealed simple goals that prioritised love, marriage and a happy ever after. It nauseated me that she prized marriage as the main goal in her life, as if there was nothing more to achieve. We had been sitting on the front steps leading to her house, just after the call for evening prayers, enjoying the cool breeze, which let us sample the aroma from their neighbour's dinner. Across from Leyla's home stood a beautiful house, like the ones of fairy tales, surrounded by ornamented steel and topped with intricate gables.

Guard stations filled each front corner, with guards patrolling the perimeter day and night. It was the home of a high-ranking official. It seemed odd that such affluence faced the home of a girl whose opportunity for education had been substituted by the daily task of washing dirty plates in the cold and dreaming of a wedding made in paradise. I spoke to Leyla about her interests — surely there must have been something she enjoyed doing besides cleaning and waiting for marriage? Did she have a hobby, or would she like to have a job outside the home, where she could earn money? Leyla's thoughts were loudly interrupted by her father's voice: "Come inside the house, girls! We don't want people talking about two troublemakers!"

We returned inside and went to the only bedroom in the house, which had a large storage closet with enough space to accommodate blankets and pillows separately. There Leyla had hidden a book with poems she had written. She was an eloquent writer and to my great surprise and relief, her poems revealed dreams that far transcended the sanctity of marriage. Leyla did have high aspirations, she simply had not met anyone who took the time to encourage her and help her believe in their viability. She needed a supporter to stimulate and nurture her determination, someone who could overlook debilitating ideas based on gender, and show her a better path to human fulfilment. In this sense, her family had a profoundly detrimental affect on Leyla. Because of her gender, their aspirations for her stopped at securing a husband. Her reality saddened me. I do not oppose marriage for people who choose it without compromising other opportunities, but Leyla had been robbed of choice. She had been forced out of school and thrown into a life of servitude in the home of her parents, only to wait for a similar life with a husband. She had not enjoyed the basic right of choice — to live her life according to her wishes instead of following her parents' demands in a society that framed her as an unpaid domestic worker. Leyla was still an adolescent and too young to consider marriage, which is far more appropriate for adults. She had her entire life ahead of her and should have had the freedom to envision plans that went beyond marriage and domesticity. I tried to explain this, but it was a difficult concept for parents to grasp. I feared they might perceive me as a bad influence or a privileged outsider, whose whims were always satisfied. This was far from the case. My parents instilled a strong sense of work and responsibility in all their children, without violating our freedom. I tried desperately to help Leyla, going so far as asking my mother to finance her secondary education, but her parents would not accept our offer. I tried to explain how important it was for Leyla to return to school so she could ensure a more fulfilling and autonomous future, but the idea was too alien and unsettled her extremely poor parents. I had always hoped to not see many children in Leyla's circumstances; meeting her was a brutal reality check, especially because this was someone whose great potential had been denied opportunity.

Literacy among women is increasing. Statistics show that an increased number of women continue to postgraduate studies, but there are some girls who do not complete their formative education because of their family's financial difficulties. This problem also affects boys. Despite these regrettable circumstances, the government has not created a state benefit to assist minors and safeguard their right to education. Leyla is an unfortunate victim because, although education is free in Kurdistan, the provision costs overwhelmed her family. In a region that does not have many job choices for adolescent girls, Leyla's future is bleak without an education.

In 2014, Leyla received a marriage proposal, which she accepted. I guess, it must have seemed like her prayers were answered because she was eager to start a family of her own. Not long after being married, we received a phone-call from her desperate mother, crying on the phone, sobbing uncontrollably, we didn't realise what had happened.

Leyla self-immolated in the kitchen. She was hospitalised and was covered in severe burns, managing to live only for three days. Her mother, and sisters explained that her husband had been abusive towards her, but Leyla only revealed these details in hospital, where she was barely able to speak. She had told her mother that she merely wanted to scare her husband by pouring gasoline on herself, and that he ignited her. Her case is still being investigated, and I have not talked about it much.

I don't know what to say, perhaps I should have done more. Why didn't she talk to me about her marriage problems? If I called her more regularly, perhaps if I visited more often, she could have seen a way out of her miserable life. It's hard for me to understand, she was strong, cheerful, and full of hope for the future. There were so many things she talked about wanting to achieve, and do after marriage.

All that was robbed form her because she didn't have a viable option that safeguarded her, secured her of backlash. It is incredibly hard for me to understand what could have led her to make that horrifying decision to self-immolate.

THE WALLET

"A good reputation is more valuable than money."

Publilius Syrus

Poverty is a nightmare. In Erbil Province it is the content of one's wallet, not achievement, that earns a person respect. Throughout the region people regard the poor with contempt. Erbil has large shopping centres, new buildings and industrial structures in development, but the poor remain poor, without any improvement in their living conditions. To observe this discrepancy more closely I visited a flea market in Erbil and interviewed local people to learn about their lives.

The flea market in Erbil is known as *Lenge* and there people buy clothes from the shipments that shop owners receive. The shops are minuscule, but all have their own air conditioning units, which produce a terrible odour that hovers in the humid air, with the sugary smell of pastries and stench of human perspiration — all unified in unbearable heat. The shops protrude from the sides of narrow tunnels where an endless number of children toil as cleaners. Children also sell popular goods, including water bottles, chewing gum and baklava (a sweet pastry made in thin layers of dough lined with honey or syrup and nuts). The child workers are usually around 9 to 12 years of age, and sometimes poorly dressed and unwashed, as evidenced from the thick dirt lodged beneath their nails. Their appearance has little effect on their demeanour, however, as they always greet customers with enthusiasm and an eager smiles. They express, in fact, a surprisingly adult business manner when enticing visitors to buy the products in the shops.

Asim Jawhar, 11, is one of the child workers of *Lenge*. He sells bottles of water and sugary drinks, which cool in a box filled with ice and water. I gave Asim 250 dinars in exchange for water and asked him if I could interview him. He seemed reluctant and looked around him cautiously, his brow forming a fearful, inquisitive arch above his honey-coloured eyes. I reassured him that the interview would not cause him trouble — I merely wanted to learn about the poorer, neglected parts of Southern Kurdistan.

Asim thought for some time. He asked who I was, where I was going to tell his story, and so on. He conducted a small interview of his own before he allowed me to switch the roles. I learned he lived with his mother and four brothers. His father had died from heart failure and his mother had since earned her living as a seamstress of traditional Kurdish dresses and nightgowns. His two younger brothers, of ages 9 and 13, still attended school, and the older two, who were 16 and 23, worked. The oldest brother was in the Peshmerge forces (equivalent to Kurdish army), which meant he was paid infrequently and occasionally summoned to accompany officials on their travels outside of Erbil Province.

Asim told me that he did not see a different future for himself; he simply wanted to manage daily life and see his younger brothers finish school to secure a better future than his own. Then he looked away to conceal tears welling in his eyes and said that sometimes his family does not have enough money to buy bread and yoghurt to eat in the morning or evening, as done by Kurdish families. He said there had been times when his brothers looked for food scraps in other people's rubbish bins. Asim then looked at me with a defeated expression, the sort one might see in an 80-year-old man who has learned that his disease is incurable, and said: "Life isn't easy, but what can we do? You write my story but then what, you go your way, live your life and forget me."

Asim's mother has diabetes and suffers from resulting neuropathy, which affects her extremities, causing her to limp. Even so, she never stops working. Asim said their extended relatives are more financially secure, but have never offered to help them. He felt disheartened, hurt by the neglect: "People don't have any mercy anymore. If they did they would help us." Asim is one of hundreds of children who work in Erbil to help support their families. To the best of my knowledge, the local government has not taken action to help them, especially with monetary assistance that would help them attend school.

Near the shop where Asim worked I met Baxtyar, a jovial man in his 20s who said he had also begun to work in Lenge when he was a child to help support his family. Baxtyar said that in the 1990s his family sold sacks of bread crumbs to buy rice. As a child and teen he had worn the same clothes to school everyday, but this mattered little because he was studying, which gave his parents immense pride. During that time Baxtyar began to work in Lenge without his parents' knowledge, to help the family with expenses. Eventually his father welcomed the decision because Baxtyar's earnings helped improve life for the family.

"It pains me to see children like Asim, but what can we do?" Baxtyar asked rhetorically, before adding: "There aren't one or two children like Asim, there are hundreds of them, they are all over the place, you can't help them all. We can't even help ourselves." I told Asim and Baxtyar that in the UK school is compulsory from ages five to 16, from which point young people can choose to work. The two workers reflected on this and smiled in amusement.

I felt silly presenting this information in a place so distant from the practices of post-industrial societies. Near Lenge there is a neighbourhood called Gilkend, which I visited with the help of Khadija, a resident who guided me in the area. As we passed the houses, she explained that the state of the doors indicated each family's income. Clean double doors in the front reflected better finances and quality of life than single doors, particularly those showing holes or general dilapidation.

During our walk through the streets of Gilkend, friendly people invited us to visit their homes. Many of these had a single bedroom without a kitchen, which some of the hosts preferred that we not photograph; but most did not object and were happy to let us take pictures. Khadija's home had two bedrooms but no electricity. Inside, the house was dark and hot. She apologised profusely about the darkness, as she placed two water glasses on a round dining table. "Sorry, I wish we had something else to offer you, but we don't. We've literally got nothing. My three sons, none of them are in school and my husband is a worker." Khadija said he did not earn stable wages, so she did domestic work to help feed the family. She would not comment on her husband's specific line of work, which could mean he worked in sanitation or waste removal — professions generally regarded unfavourably.

Khadija was a slender woman with large, bright, beautiful eyes and a generous smile. Her presence was strong and her expression urgent. Sitting before her in the hot, dark room, I felt sharp pain in my chest, as if needles were stuck to my heart. "Do you want to start a petition for a government program that helps children stay in school?" I asked, at a loss for alternatives."Where can I sign?" she responded bluntly, with a tone of optimism. I told Khadija that many European countries, including Germany and the UK, have established funds to assist poor children. These programs offer subsidised housing and financial and social support to the children and their families. In this way children of modest means do not have to work to eat, but can use their time to attend school and access a path of healthier opportunities, I explained to Khadija.

When we parted, Khadija shook my hands firmly, kissed my cheeks and blessed me with prayers. I told her I would try to persuade people to help me campaign for a children's cause and motivate the local government to take direct action. I reminded her that alone I cannot change the present conditions, but with support anything is possible. Still, I cautioned her to not expect overnight change. The social problems and poverty of Gilkend could not be fixed in one day—it would take years for authorities and organisations to ameliorate conditions for local residents.

In the days following my visit to Gilkend I studied a map of Erbil and tried to decide how to begin a petition. At that point I had only three months left in the region before my return to London, but I was determined to get as many signatures as possible before leaving. I understood that to achieve anything with my idea, I needed family support. Their help was particularly essential, as they have often warned me to be cautious and not get too political or involved in matters that exceed my resources. I have always understood that my family prioritises my well-being, but when it comes to helping others in need, I feel compelled by a moral obligation before God. I cannot turn a blind eye when the poor starve and live in the dark, while their children miss their right to learn.

Not long after, I visited a shop in Erbil and photocopied 100 petition sheets, each with ample space for people's names, signatures, addresses and phone numbers. The petition respectfully asks Mr Masoud Barzani, president of the Kurdistan Region, to initiate a financial support program for poor children, so that they can remain in school and have enough clothing and food. My parents, relatives, neighbours and associates were the first to sign the children's petition. Most were happy to sign, but some people, despite signing, said it was a waste of time and I should not occupy myself with issues that cannot be fixed.

Although Kurdish people have for centuries helped each other in times of difficulty, Kurdistan does not have the structured system of volunteering found in western cultures. Local Kurds are reluctant to perform favours in return for nothing. Moreover, the prospect of knocking on doors does not appeal to them. But I did not collect signatures for personal gain; I campaigned on behalf of Kurdish children who desperately needed help to enjoy their basic rights. There is a higher principle here, so I worked everyday to collect as many signatures as possible, hoping the hard work will benefit the right people. I cannot think of a better gain than seeing children rescued from debilitating poverty.

When I collected sufficient signatures, I was able to meet the former Minister of Labour and Social Affairs. Asos Najib Abdullah told me that the Kurdistan Regional Government simply did not have sufficient budget to cover this initiatives, despite illustrating public interest for the initiative. She dismissed the campaign with little regard to its goals, and it was quite demoralising at the time.

THE HELP

*"Remember no one can make you feel inferior
without your consent."*

Eleanor Roosevelt

My grandmother is 70 years old, frail and thin. For many years she has employed a domestic worker named Sana, she has become a close family friend. When Sana has any problems she discusses them openly with my grandmother and aunts. On one such occasion she said her sons have often mistreated her, to the point of physical battery. Although she is elderly, Sana pays half of the US $400 monthly rent of the home she shares with her two adult sons. This means that each of her sons only pays one quarter of the total rent, and since

Sana earns US$200 per month, she is left with no money after paying her unfair share.

On one occasion her sons did not contribute their share of the rent, Sana insisted that they give her the money only to receive a brutal beating in return. My family was outraged, but my grandmother was not sure how to deal with the situation, given that in Kurdistan poor women have such limited recourse. Sana's injuries had left her severely bruised and some of her wounds required stitching at the hospital. Despite the severity of the attack, Sana did not report the incident to the police because she felt ashamed that her sons had assaulted her. I did not discuss the incident with Sana because of my young age at the time and an inability to relate to the trauma, but I know that the entire family was enormously supportive to Sana.

Statistics for violence against women are not fully documented in Erbil province. It is thus extremely difficult for local organisations to quantify it and design a specific course of action to reduce attacks on women. Nonetheless, it is clear that legislation is not enough to challenge the social stigma that comes with reporting domestic violence.

Kurdistan needs a social revolution that will enlighten people about gender roles and stop men from abusing female relatives. Brutality, whether physical or psychological, only harms Kurdish people — it does not protect anybody's honour.

Violence against women is not exclusive to Kurdish women or the Middle East. Estimates show that thousands of women experience violence in the UK, and various organisations have reported a rise in the number of rapes and murders of women. The general statistics are frightening, but they keep activists and social workers informed and help them provide effective care to victims and design prevention programs. The absence of figures in Kurdistan does not point to a smaller incidence of attacks on women; it only shows that the region lacks the means to measure violence.

Violence against women tends to be motivated by issues of control and restriction. To reduce this trend, a society must have the proper mechanisms in place to help women escape domestic violence and abusive relationships. Shelters for battered women and organisations that offer counselling and job skills training are extremely critical in the effort to keep women safe in a manner that is productive and dignified. Survivors of violence do not need institutional confinement and isolation from society, as oftentimes arranged in Kurdistan; they need mental health care in a way that does not stigmatise or ostracise them from society. Thus far I have not seen proper mental health facilities for survivors of violence in Kurdistan and this is necessary because it helps women rebuild self-esteem and reintegrate in society.

In discussions of violence, people often overlook how much of it is instigated by women against women. This is an insidious phenomenon of patriarchy that we cannot ignore, particularly as it does not damage women directly, but obstructs their reasoning enough to turn them into misogynist agents. Sana, the woman who worked for my grandmother, is not the only victim of violence in her family. Rezan, a 33-year-old activist, says her mother beat her severely when, as a teenager, she stood outside her home to avoid feeling bored or depressed inside. She says life is different now, and mothers no longer beat their daughters like that, but they still use abusive language to control them.

People seem to struggle with the idea of changing old habits, perhaps because patriarchy is a social disease that manifests in both men and women.

HUMAN RIGHTS

"To deny people their human rights is to challenge their very humanity."

Nelson Mandela

Women are not the only group whose rights are ignored in Southern Kurdistan. The area has a general problem with human rights violations, although it also allows people to challenge abusers. For example, Dr Rebwar Fatah went on strike with his colleagues at Erbil teaching Hospital to challenge negligence towards patients. The region does not have policies in place that allow patients to demand compensation for medical negligence. It still lacks laws that guard specific rights. However, strikes by doctors are often dismissed, and they can face consequences from their respective healthcare departments.

Kurdistan's modernisation process is young, and people are in the early stages of developing a viable legal sector. These efforts have brought forth cases never seen before in the area, such as those guarded under privacy and defamation laws in western systems.

Some people suggest that we should not focus on women's rights as exclusive gender rights, but as human rights. However, including women's rights in general human rights is more useful in movements that guard the rights of men and women as people. A retrospective examination shows that both sexes have only occasionally spoken against the specific violations of women's rights; while most people stand readily in favour of human rights. The people who have organised protests to support women's rights and expose violations have mostly been women, and they have done so without significant male support. For many questionable reasons, societal structures force people to categorise women's rights under the umbrella of human rights. This practice of sub-categorisation also applies to children and other disadvantaged groups in Kurdistan. One cannot help but wonder how they came to rest at a disadvantage, but I suspect it relates to the same inequality that sustains the quota system that recruits women for parliament in the region.

The lack of interest in women's political inclusion effectively supports a problematic quota system that allows any female candidate from established political parties to gain a seat in parliament. This means that not all women appointed to parliament are qualified for the job. As for female candidates running independently, they rarely get far, unless they have the considerable wealth needed to launch an efficient campaign. This may explain why the region has yet to elect a parliamentary female member who ran independently. Evidently the political system in the area has much to learn, perhaps even from Middle Eastern states flawed with nepotism.

To empower women in all sectors of society we must first establish balance in institutions controlled by men, which sustain patriarchal values. This shift must include an effort to make political, social and academic organisations more receptive to female leadership. Such genuine effort would eliminate the practice of placing random women in high positions to satisfy political agendas. Kurdistan needs honest, independent candidates whose records show an active concern for women's advancement in society. Such candidates need not be female to perform well as politicians who honour justice and progress. I am certain that any open-minded woman would support a male parliamentary member whose actions honoured the specific rights of women and human beings in general. For example, such dedicated MP would support the expansion of shelters for women and children fleeing domestic violence; and would promote social and financial reform for women. He would be a political innovator and champion human causes. Not only would such great politician try to include more qualified women in government, he would also create programs that help working people build businesses. The hard working people of Kurdistan whose labour ensures survival, but no substantial wealth, are the ones who need help to progress.

In Kurdistan, struggling and successful

women have been indoctrinated by a social tradition of patriarchal values. This structure gives the women of top positions little motivation to help women with less fortunate lives. They care about their success, and make considerable effort to maintain it, an achievement that gives other countries the idea that in Kurdistan women have achieved equality with men. Additionally, outsiders have begun to perceive these women as the altruistic kind, who try continuously to help those in need, but the reality seems entirely different. Women who gain political power in Kurdistan seem to forgo any attempts to help other capable women rise through the ranks of power. Concerned with preserving their own status, they develop a rigid attitude of self preservation that cuts time or willingness to develop social rehabilitation. This style is reminiscent of the Thatcher years, when Britain marvelled in the power of the Iron Lady — a woman known for her intelligence and ruthlessness. Thatcher's success as a three-term prime minister likely depended on the unwavering approach that earned her the moniker. History books often cite her feminism, but I wonder why a woman with such power did not include more female leaders in her cabinet. Is feminism not a practical effort to provide equal opportunities to men and women? The present situation in Kurdish politics seems to follow the troubling steps of the Thatcher method — rise as a female leader in the world of men, but share not the podium with other women.

Women must be over 25 years old to run for parliament in Kurdistan. The age requirement works against them, given that women in the region typically marry in their early 20s (earlier generations married younger). Motherhood soon follows marriage and by the time local women reach the age of 25 they are considerably occupied with childcare, household chores and work outside the home. Such social circumstances make it impossible for average working class women to attempt a political career in parliament; and leave a psychological mark of patriarchal custom. In many ways our lives make us who we are, and after years of living a certain lifestyle people often lose sight of greater possibilities. Thus in Kurdistan the younger, unmarried, childless activists with the necessary time to participate in Kurdish politics, do not because of the age requirement. These are the women who could share insight from the perspective of a younger generation in tune with contemporary social problems — and the ones who do not fear change and possibility.

When we combine the aforementioned conditions, we find a sociopolitical landscape that does not support the ascension of women. So why have female politicians not recognised these problems and tried to help other women in Kurdistan access professional opportunities? The consensus seems to be that the more success a woman attains in the region, the less pleasant and receptive she becomes. Obviously it is wrong to base conclusions on generalisations derived from gossip; but I have examples based on personal experience. During my work in Kurdistan I tried many times to arrange meetings with female members of parliament, but each attempt brought me only excuses justified by busy schedules and lack of time. On the other hand, male MPs were forthcoming and willing to discuss local politics. The pattern of insufficient collaboration among female politicians in Kurdistan can also extend to some local activists. By contrast, it takes only a few phone calls to see twenty male activists materialise, ready to help support a cause. I saw this first hand in the summer of 2012 while organising a child benefit campaign in Erbil. Throughout the efforts to make logistical arrangements for the children's benefit, I became aware that it was difficult to motivate female activists to help during this period, although as noted earlier, there exists greater collaboration amongst activists in recent times. During the campaign, many offered disbelief as their reason for lack of participation.

It is difficult to understand why so many women in Kurdistan fail to support each other, but from my interviews, I learned that they are less likely than men to support female politicians and television anchors. The women's responses that I interviewed reflect a critical stance toward the female leaders and presenters, whose demeanour and purpose they criticised unsparingly. Their answers reveal more cultural stereotype than fact, given that in Kurdistan it is men who usually commit public fault. In fact, history shows that men were always the chief culprits of civil war in the area.

Clearly they could use input from women to establish a peaceful society, but women in Kurdistan do not seem ready for the collaborative work required in the region. The power of patriarchy has become so embedded in the general psyche that even intelligent women have come to defend its value. Unfortunately this social problem isolates women with great potential from each other, and diminishes the possibilities for political change. Women's lack of mutual support is costing the region more than it can afford to lose.

As touched on earlier, Kurdistan's general elections follow a gender quota because women have terrible difficulty gaining parliamentary seats. The truth is that without this quota system women would not gain many seats. Consider the following, if people elect the men of said parties because they support their policies and principles, why do they not elect the same parties' female candidates whose views are identical? I cannot help but conclude that people in Kurdistan either distrust women's ability or feel uncomfortable seeing them in high positions of power. This would explain why the region needs a quota system that robs capable women of the opportunity to earn a job on merit alone. In its current state the quota system seems to do more harm than good, as it allows mainstream political parties to appoint women they can control. It seems like high end patriarchy.

I believe life would be easier for women if they chose to rise above oppressive values to work together. I understand that education and exposure are essential to motivate a person toward justice; but at a certain point nothing is more powerful than choice and it is this I find lacking in Kurdistan. Women are not making the choice to stand together and build a better world for everyone. Patriarchal systems have existed in human societies for many generations, but the time has come to alleviate men's burden and include women in leadership to balance decisions. To achieve this I believe women everywhere, but especially in Kurdistan and other developing regions, must stand together. They can honour a healthier tradition by supporting local work and charities that benefit disadvantaged women and children, and thus society in the long term. Such efforts should dispense with discouragement masked as tradition. In the new millennium cooperation among women really ought to discard archaic phrases that use gender to argue inability.

Unfortunately the current reality is markedly different, as confirmed by the words of Trifa Arifa, a nursing home and orphanage volunteer in Southern Kurdistan: "Young women can be selfish and critical of each other. They hate it when other women are successful. Everybody here is jealous, but the men criticise what other men do, not who they are." Indeed jealousy is a human emotion that manifests in men and women, but at times more destructively so in local women. This is rather unfortunate since jealousy and criticism hurt women more than men, who enjoy more professional opportunities and social freedoms than women. Jealousy thus can destroy women's lives, but seems to have no significant impact on the quality of life for local men.

THE ORPHANAGE

"The best of the houses is the house where an orphan gets love and kindness."
Prophet Muhammad (Peace be upon him)

Orphaned children in Kurdistan live in unimaginable conditions. Their caretakers are not trained professionally for their jobs, and few understand why it is important to communicate daily with the children. They focus mainly on maintenance and emergency tasks, such as calling medical help when a child falls and breaks a bone. In 2012 friends and I were given permission to visit local orphanages on Thursdays. The orphanage system places children of both genders together until they reach age 10, at which time they are separated. During one of our visits to the mixed children's house, we encountered a chaotic scene. Caretakers sat on sofas while children as young as two moved randomly in all directions. One of them cried incessantly because "Aya hit me." This child had a broken finger. Nearby two recently arrived children — a brother and a sister — sat quietly together. Their journey to the orphanage had began when their mother died through self-immolation. They were poorly dressed, their faces smeared with dirt, mucus dripped from their noses. The boy, whose birth date had not been established, appeared to be under two years old. Hoger, as they called him, was soiled with urine and would remain so throughout the three hours we spent at the orphanage that day. Our attempts to convince the staff to change the poor child or provide materials for us to do it for them went unheard. Each time we mentioned Hoger they eyed him heartlessly and ignored the ailing toddler.

Despite the sad events in his life, Hoger seemed like a determined child. On several occasions he demonstrated strong will and a desire to persevere. For example, when three of the orphanage girls returned from school carrying chocolate, Hoger approached them and, unable to speak, raised his hand toward the bar. One of the girls broke a small piece and gave it to him. Hoger inspired generosity around him. Even a noted house bully shared water with him, although he got soaked since he was was too little to hold the bottle as he drank. Still, Hoger refused help from others and tried to control the situation. He willed autonomy, and when this failed, he cried or ran to his sister, who was about four years older. Hoger was cautious around outsiders. When my friend Ashna Shareff gave him her camera and I presented my cell phone to gain his trust, Hoger was not impressed. Unfamiliar faces made him uneasy and he often cuddled in the arms of his young sister, who had become his protector by tragic circumstance. Equally tragic was the fact that this girl had fulfilled that role at an age when she herself needed protection. Hamdia believed their father would return for them some day. Sadly we heard from the staff that the children's father had gone to Baghdad in search of a new wife and wished for no contact with Hamdia and Hoger.

Not surprisingly the orphanage children

seemed sad and withdrawn. We tried to engage them in activities with no success until we discovered they liked to draw. Through their drawings they expressed how they felt. Sometimes they asked us to draw specific images of houses and people. In their requests the children communicated their needs. A girl named Helene, for example, asked if we could draw the following on her sheet of paper: A mother, a doctor father, a younger sister, a jump rope and a smiling moon. We obliged much to her delight. Helene's wishes were simple and basic; she wanted a family, love and a place to call home. She desired affection and safety — she craved the presence of parents who could care for her needs. This need for family was immense in the children. Nearly all of them revealed this in their drawings, which were filled with images of father and mother figures. The orphanage staff did not have enough activities to fill the children's days, but worse, the general neglect was palpable. Simple activities like drawing or sharing stories did not exist in this orphanage. The children spent days caring for themselves and each other in their filthy rooms with minimal adult supervision.

On average each room had four beds, some of which were dirty, with sheets bearing the marks of pens and stains. The disarray and filth made a disturbing scene. Apart from the beds, the rooms lacked an area where the children could sit and play. The main room, where the television exercised full control of the staff, also had no appropriate play or study area for the children. One of the staff members was pregnant and remained in her seat, glued to the screen, throughout our visit. While she watched her show, a little girl cried behind a nearby sofa. I resisted the urge to take the child into my arms and console her so that I could note how long this woman—soon to bring her own child into the world—would ignore the sobs. With heartache I timed the crying; it lasted what seemed like 20 minutes until another staff member approached the child.

The main problem affecting children like Hoger is not one of governmental funding, but one of irresponsible allocation. Local officials designate funds to support orphaned and abandoned children, but the employees governing the funds do not know how to govern them properly. This results in insufficient resources to sustain comprehensive annual care for the children. Lacking money to manage the orphanages properly, employees sooner or later find themselves understaffed and lacking resources. The end result is fatigue and acute neglect toward the least deserving — the children under their care. But how do staff members get to this point? Their own neglect may help explain the situation. Although children without parents present an urgent challenge for society, in Kurdistan they are deposited and forgotten at orphanages in the care of workers equally forgotten by society. The workers' social isolation in conjunction with absent media attention create a dangerous concoction of festering neglect and apathy. Fundamentally it is not more money that will solve the problem of neglect, but humanity. If we are to succeed in addressing the disgraceful problem of neglected children, we must begin by publicly acknowledging the existence of orphans, and training their caretakers. We cannot simply look away because it is too painful to learn the story of children like Hamdia. Our pity is only a convenient reaction to avoid responsibility, and as such it is completely useless to abandoned children.

As human beings, we have a moral obligation to extend our help to those less fortunate, particularly when such people are children, the most vulnerable of our societies. Obviously social work cannot exist without financial resources, but humanity goes further, and without it the management of resources collapses and situations become unbearable, as in the orphanages of Kurdistan.

The young children's orphanage had an overwhelming smell of urine. I understand that the staff may have felt tired from caring for so many children, but they could have maintained a cleaner environment for the sake of health and hygiene. Bodily fluids are known to spread disease, particularly among young children who use their fingers and mouths to experience the world. Poor hygiene in orphanages is not only a bad example for children, it is potentially deadly. When children live and sleep in filth day after day, year after year, their health declines. Since children are the future of any nation, such conditions weaken development in Kurdistan. As compassionate beings, we ought to accept the challenge of educating our people to be kinder and more humane with all children -

orphaned or privileged. Perhaps we can begin by publicising the plight of poor children to inspire compassion from orphanage workers, whose jobs include the opportunity to change young lives. These people do not earn much, so public recognition of their work and respect for their roles could motivate them to treat the children better.

The second orphan house we visited housed children older than 12. On arrival we found a girl scrubbing floors. Newly arrived, she had come to live in the orphanage because her family could not care for her. Performing domestic chores is an important life skill, but I wonder how much of it paid employees actually perform at orphanages when young residents do so much of the work. I worry whether these children do more chores than acceptable for their age. Unfortunately it was not possible to determine this during our visits because the children are cautious around staff members and reveal only loose fragments of their lives. I understand their caution because I can interview them, collect information and leave; but they do not have the same privilege - they must live in the orphanages and interact with staff members, who have immense power over the direction of their lives. Thus my work could have a direct affect on the children's lives - for better or for worse.

When I consider the orphanage situation in Southern Kurdistan, I realise that the region suffers from a lack of non-profit organisations and citizen initiative. In most developed nations, these efforts are critical to the management of social problems, such as domestic violence, child welfare and poverty. Kurdistan is now in the beginning of a transitory phase, which provides ample opportunity for people to make changes that benefit the region. It is during such times that we must master the courage to challenge systems that oppress women, neglect children and force men to guard patriarchal values. We can still call on the government for more participation in this respect, but at some point we must own responsibility for the society we represent. Governmental policy impacts society, but social change begins with individual behaviour. Great power rests in the hands of people who recognise that honour lies in justice and the social progress of all human beings.

During our visits to Kurdish orphanages,

friends and I received boxes full of presents from people – citizens of all corners of the globe — eager to help the children. Volunteers Ashna Shareff, Nawroz Sinjari, Sazan Mandalawi and I sorted the gifts according to age group and delivered them to the children at the Malle Khanda (House of Smiles) orphanage. The children were joyous when they saw us arrive with the boxes, but unfortunately the staff would lock the toys in a glass cupboard to prevent them from "making a mess."

The event motivated us to have a discussion with the orphanage administrator and volunteer our time to create fun, learning activities for the children. I remember vividly an incident that occurred in the house of the younger children. The orphanage accommodates 400 children, but because some alternate residence with relatives or paid guardians, the daily number present varies. One day people visiting the older children's section left remaining gifts for three of the younger girls. Unfortunately their kind act left several girls empty handed and one crying. Rather upset, one child buried her head in one of the main room sofas and cried for a prolonged period. Her grief did not seem to affect the staff, who continued to chat unmoved by the child's sobs. They believed that ignoring the child would eventually stop the crying.

That may have been true, but the reasoning troubled me, as the child was hurt and in desperate need of affection. A hug from her caretakers would have been humane and consoling, whereas their indifference reinforced neglect.

When the other volunteers and I left for the day, the young child, Isra, was still crying. We had shown her a teddy bear in attempts to ease her sadness, but Isra continued to cry with great grief. Her simple wish had been to receive new clothes and one pair of shoes, but we could not grant it without doing the same for the other children in the orphanage houses. Doing so would have displayed favouritism, a practice that deeply hurts children. Ashna, one of the volunteers present that day, and I discussed the situation at length and reached the same conclusion from every angle — we must treat all children at the orphanage with equal kindness and generosity; and because there are hundreds of them, there can be absolutely no exceptions. If we buy specific goods for one child, we must be prepared to do same for all 399 others. We had noted this carefully when we learned earlier that week that the donated boxes of toys did not have enough dolls for all the girls.

On the fourth of July, following generous support from many people, we filled a minibus with 22 children from the orphanage and drove to Erbil International Airport for a short adventure. The initial plan was to take only 10 children, so that we could manage the trip without causing disturbance at the airport, but when they heard about the plan, the children became extremely excited and persuaded us to take more of them. How could we resist their spontaneous strategy, which consisted mainly in begging and occupying the vehicle? As they packed the minibus, the children smiled anxiously in anticipation of seeing an airplane for the first time. The orphanage supervisor relented and the number of our little companions grew from 10 to 22 in a matter of minutes. Our delight matched the children's joy.

During the journey to the airport we clapped hands and sang nursery rhymes and the Kurdish national anthem. Everyone was happy and the children's eyes sparkled with renewed hope. It was clear that these young travellers had begun to believe in the possibility of their dreams. We felt grateful to be in a position to help the children experience life outside the orphanage. Exposure to variety at a young age can inspire people to create a focused path for their lives. We were happy to give a little bit of this potential genesis to the orphanage children, whose enthusiasm multiplied as we approached the airport. As our bus passed a plane in flight, they pointed to the windows and exclaimed with utter joy: "There it is! It's a plane! Look at it! We're going there!"

Once inside the airport, a tremendously kind member of staff gave us a tour, so the children could learn how such a facility works. The little adventurers watched with great curiosity as airport workers interacted with travellers, received their luggage and directed them to security areas. The children were mesmerised by the process. With great excitement they held each other's hands and asked us continuously about their turn to board a plane. Soon a plane at a nearby gate emptied of the last passengers and all but two children 'boarded' with unstoppable enthusiasm. Two of them, fearful of the large aircraft, began to cry. We reassured them that the plane was not dangerous and their fears eventually transformed into eager curiosity. Inside the aircraft, the children ran from seat to seat, searching for the best window view. They sat, fastened their seat belts and listened attentively to our description of what pilots do in cockpits to fly airplanes. They seemed awestruck and asked us to photograph them in their seats, which we did, of course.

After a few snapshots, it became clear that the children were ready for more than an airport tour. Wanting to experience an even more ambitious adventure, they urged us to fly somewhere. With arms stretched upward they giggled and exclaimed: "Let's go to Europe! We want to fly!" But it would not be so this time, as within minutes our time on the aircraft had come to an end. The children unbuckled their seat belts and presented the captain with a beautiful appreciation poster they had prepared for him at the orphanage. Outside, passengers waited their turn to board the plane.

As we exited the plane we noticed Razhan, a

four-year-old girl, crouched behind a seat in giggles, hiding from the group. Razhan had decided that she was going to fly, and it took us some time to convince her differently. The return bus ride to the orphanage was filled with the sound of music and excited little voices speaking simultaneously, each with a story or theory about the journey. I looked around, absorbing the moment, and saw my joy reflected in the faces of the other volunteers. They were all tired, but had revealing smiles etched on their faces. We understood that the orphanage children had experienced something remarkable that would forever change their view of the world.

The standard of care towards orphans and those supervising them has improved significantly since 2012. This is largely due to local efforts to provide better care to orphans, but unfortunately one phenomenon continues to exist, which should be curtailed. Many local volunteers are visiting these orphanages, sometimes to provide presents, or fund the orphan's dinner trips at high-end restaurants. Consequently, they post pictures of these trips with the orphans on their social networking sites, without blurring their faces.

Orphans do not have the capacity to consent, even if they agree to their pictures being uploaded on Facebook, they're simply not at an age where they can make that life-long decision. Volunteers should behave more responsibly, and I'm not merely saying this to absolve myself from responsibility on this issue. During my trips in 2012, I took several pictures with orphans, and we used it on our social networking sites, but those pictures have since been taken down, with an explanation.

Whenever I have attempted to rectify this grave mistake that we made, volunteers often respond with criticism and are offended. We must be vigilant to act in the interests of vulnerable children, and this means the administration within the orphanage itself must ensure that random volunteers do not visit for merely taking selfies with orphans, boosting their own egoistical need to flaunt their humanitarian activities on various social networking sites.

ERBIL CITY'S FIRST FEMINIST CLUB

*"In the future, there will be no female leaders.
There will just be leaders."*

Sheryl Sandberg

Much happened in Erbil during the summer of 2012. June had marked the first feminist meeting among a group of young men and women, which sparked a small scale movement. For a long time I had dreamed of a local feminist organisation that would teach young Kurdish girls to develop strength and self-reliance in the new Kurdistan. Fully aware that education does not equate to liberation, I tried to welcome girls of all social classes to our first meeting. I understood that the city had several youth groups that encourage young people to participate in civil society, but none of them seemed to address the status of women in Kurdistan. Ashna, with whom I volunteered at the orphanages, and I made some calls and now a group of young people sat together for an informal chat. Ashna helped lead the meeting, which made perfect sense as she is a resident of Erbil city, who believes in women's equal participation in society. This first discussion in an unremarkable location comprised of three men and four women, including Ashna and me.

Some of the attendees arrived early, others left late. Our group may have lacked perfect organisation, but it had something essential: a beginning. On that day we agreed to meet weekly at local cafes to discuss women's rights over a soft drink or two. During our meetings we discussed how people treat women locally and in neighbouring countries, but we focused mainly on the situation in Erbil. Everyone expressed unique ideas, but as a group we shared similar goals, even if some people perceived feminism as a misguided approach to women's liberation. Unfortunately, the meetings did not last for long, and when I left Erbil city, no one continued the initiative.

In the first two meetings, our conversations lasted hours, and throughout the period religion featured prominently. Some of the men present tried to use religion to block our proposals, which did not surprise me since many people in the area use religion to justify tradition that keeps women behind men. For example, clerics frequently cite women in their Friday sermons about "the national epidemic of immoral behaviour and corruption." Fortunately their interpretation of immorality is preposterous, given that it condemns basic freedoms like social interaction between men and women. Some clerics are broadminded, but most promote this sickening habit of wanting to control women.

Some clerics are also clever in how they select their villain; they appear apolitical (which keeps them in good graces with politicians) and remain consistently critical of women. The fact that they publicly judge women — who are in a weaker social position—magnifies their bullying behaviour and lack of piety. More seriously, these clerics plant oppressive ideas in the minds of thousands in attempts to stunt Kurdish progress. What good can come in a society that ignores the abilities of one gender? How dare men of cloth desecrate scripture and falsely indoctrinate people to attack women's rights?

Despite instances of endemic ugliness and coercion, Kurdish feminists must find a way to build constructive communication with clerics. This may seem monumental and nerve-testing, but it is one of the most essential tasks in the Kurdish feminist movement. clerics have power; they inspire and motivate people to take action. Right now they are using this power to reinforce customs that oppress women and hold back social evolution. As feminists, we must use reason to inspire these men of God to use their power for good. We must encourage clerics to part with patriarchy and honour Islam in contemporary society. Mosques, churches, temples and other places of worship must not blame or condemn women for moral decay. Instead these sacred spaces ought to uphold the rights of women and guide people to support a world based on equal rights for men and women.

During the first feminist meeting in Erbil we

discussed the situation of adolescent girls, most of whom must obey a curfew while boys of the same age roam freely without restrictions. Local families take extra care to monitor girls' whereabouts and behaviour 24 hours a day. Young women never seem to have a free moment to express themselves away from the watchful gaze of their families. This rigid type of social control seems to also affect young professionals in the public eye. Despite being women, the latter tend to support the patriarchal values that impede their very success. At our meeting two men attributed these factors to "Kurdish culture" and argued that we must respect the local "customs." These were bright men who — like many others before them — seemed to relinquish logic in the presence of culture, even if culture abused women. I wondered, how did the word culture come to legitimise misogyny?

Today in many places throughout Kurdistan people interpret certain behaviours as evidence of women's liberation. For example, if a woman walks in public without a headscarf, wears a short skirt or a low cut blouse others may perceive her as a feminist. This is a mistake. Fashion alone is not a credible representative of feminism, and less clothing does not equate to liberation. Moreover, one woman's personal choice of dress in no way represents the choices or freedom of other women. In the case of Kurdistan it so happens that the women exposing more flesh are also affected by the traditional values that demand leadership from men and subjugation from women. Great expectations fall upon Kurdish women, who must show devotion and purity, and remain utterly insignificant in authority. The density of misguided Kurdish feminism is troubling and embarrassing: people label female professionals who socialise with male colleagues as either feminist or with overtly liberal views. At the root of this inaccurate - and shallow - perception of feminism lies the glorification of wealth and consumerism. I worry that so many in Kurdistan have come to perceive the power to buy as a sign of liberation.

In reality some local women seem to be moving further away from feminism; and Kurdistan's struggle between tradition and modernisation is developing at different speeds among people. For example, some women ignore traditional etiquette and dress according to their will, but these women usually come from a privileged group of wealthy, prominent families. Such women can afford to defy social norms because they enjoy a certain degree of impermeability in a society of class distinctions. On the other hand, the women of working class families do not have the privilege of choice; they must abide by the hard rules of local traditions, which limit women's expression and force them to conform to such ideals.

Despite being a long way from enforcing social and political equality between the sexes, Kurdistan has made commendable strides. For example there is a marked difference between now and 2004, when the places available for women to meet friends or colleagues were still few. The region now has dozens of places for young people to hang-out that were not previously available. Such clientele, however, tend to be comprised of affluent young women. Poorer girls, who lack money and status, still remain under the heavy shadow of patriarchy. Still, there is improvement, even if we can only observe it among upper classes. Erbil is changing and local women seem ready for the freedom it brings. I guess their challenge now is to extend an invitation to less privileged women to join them as they enjoy the benefits. That said, women's rights in Kurdistan ought to go far past the joyous occasion of sipping tea in public places. Full equality means equal rights in law, at work, in homes, on streets, in politics, finance, medicine and any industry or situation imaginable. To achieve this, the women of Kurdistan need to become assertive and honour justice.

Kurdish culture teaches women from an early age that they are different from boys. Parents, relatives, teachers, friends, communities, all project this difference onto children in the form of measured privilege. Little girls learn that boys can speak loudly and laugh heartily, but they must not. They see their mothers home late in evenings while their fathers go out to see friends. They learn about their older brothers' conquests, while their parents guard their sisters with utter care to ensure marriageability. In this light girls grow, one day becoming the bearers of the very values that sustain their social and psychological confinement. The cycle shows that the people of Kurdistan need more than access to institutional education; they need a social revolution that begins in the home. That said, it is important to note that not all homes are alike, and Kurdistan does have progressive families who teach little boys and girls to seek goals with equal measure. Although they are part of a greater culture, Kurdish families have unique family subcultures that follow particular rules. As in other cultures, this diversity enriches Kurdistan, but in the local environment of strict tradition it also brings envy among women. This happens because whereas some families allow girls to spend time outside the home and develop friendships with young people of both genders, most would not even consider allowing such freedom. When the majority of girls in a town miss this experience of freedom—which they regard as a luxury—they begin to resent the girls who have it. This resentment expands in the form of support for a patriarchal system that pushes girl against girl and woman against woman. Herein may lie the jealousy factor touched on earlier, which motivates grown women to badmouth and criticise those in the public eye. I suppose human nature compels us to desire the best, and when the best seems available only to some, we surrender to anger and destruction.

Alternatively, the disgruntled may choose calculated rebellion in place of gossip and pettiness. This could be possible in Kurdistan, if women refuse to relinquish power to men and decide to not resent successful women. With thoughtful alliance and organisation, local women could create an environment that offers them the right to exercise free will. To reach this stage, women must first shift their devotion from men to themselves and collapse the faulty foundation of patriarchy. Only in this way can true freedom come to women in Kurdistan and provide them a full life as equal members of a thriving society. People will then understand that feminism lies not in outer appearance or extravagance, but in the commitment to honour a just society. In its totality, freedom transcends the superficiality of personal attire and the condemnation of others to penetrate all sectors of society and create opportunities for all people. This includes the availability of leadership roles for women, but also the simple act of communication between the sexes (which some families in Kurdistan have used as a reason to murder women in the past). Real feminism gives women the chance to feel useful and dignified outside the confines of their homes—without having to fear repercussions.

CANCER

"The fear of death follow from the fear of life. A man who lives fully is prepared to die at any time."

Mark Twain

During my time in Kurdistan I had an eye infection that lasted a week. When the redness and swelling began to subside, I resumed interviewing women in the poorer areas of Erbil province. At that time I learned that a close friend from my university in London had succumbed to cancer at the age of 23, only a few months after the initial diagnosis. It has been difficult to accept that Hakimah lost her life in the pearl of adulthood. I think of her often, not with crushing sadness, but with renewed determination to support justice for the disadvantaged and marginalised. Hakimah believed in the possibility of a world where people honour character and resist the misinterpretations of religion or ethnicity. Her wisdom, which manifested as innocence, inspired me to do what I can to improve our world. I miss Hakimah, her unimposing mentorship, her selflessness and the enthusiasm she held when listening to people. Her generosity was unconditional, she seemed to find meaning and satisfaction in the act of giving.

Many times I saw Hakimah walk around the school campus, basket full of pamphlets in hand, encouraging students to sponsor charities. She was equally committed in her efforts to distribute knowledge, and often invited speakers to present lectures on philosophy, literature, theology, politics and sociology. Hakimah's life is inspirational because it shows that with great heart comes effortless will and great achievement. In her short time alive she helped and inspired people to participate in public service. The gratitude so many felt for her efforts was clear at her funeral service, which many people attended to bid farewell. They filled the mosque, some in shock, but most in awe of Hakimah. Men, women, old, young, rich, poor, all stood with eyes moist, but bright in the certainty that someone precious had touched their lives. Hakimah's female classmates, in particular, displayed a remarkable expression of gratitude — she had convinced them that they could be strong women.

I have yet to meet another young woman like Hakimah, whose selflessness did so much to help the poor and empower women. I wish it were not so, particularly in Kurdistan where there is a great need for conscientious activists. Repeatedly I have observed that young women do not seem interested in engaging social and political causes. This may be related to the lack of encouragement they receive from older people, as evidenced in a blunt comment someone once threw at me: "What business do you, as a young girl, have in the world of politics?" This attitude seems prevalent throughout Kurdistan and I fear it misguides girls from the time they are born. No one seems to tell them that they live in a world of opportunity where they can set goals and formulate action plans. They grow in this darkness only to pass the torch of discouragement to the next generation of girls. Such insidious patriarchy places thousands of women and girls on the idle margins of society, where neither voice nor will can develop to drive change.

To treat this serious social problem in Kurdistan, we must first teach people to stop idolising men just because they are male. We must motivate progression away from the belief that only men can validate a woman's worth. Men and women are equally important, and marriage does not have to be essential in conferring humanity upon women. I do not disqualify love or devalue marriage, but I believe that girls should not have to grow believing that this union must be their greatest achievement in life. In Kurdistan, where married life follows the rigours of patriarchal tradition, women almost always find themselves disillusioned with the reality of marriage. Although most spend their childhood and adolescence dreaming of the perfect gentleman who will dazzle them with romance, soon after their wedding they learn that they have entered an institution of bondage.

As wives, many women from poorer backgrounds lack authority and generally live secluded from social activities. In most cases, married life brings less freedom to women than the limitations they endured in the home of their parents. The reality facing married women in poor households are incredibly difficult, and often not talked about within feminist circles. Additionally, as offspring arrive, married women become increasingly occupied at home and removed from public life.

Together, these circumstances disconnect women from the inner strength that inspires ambition or social involvement. By the time they reach their late 20s most women in Kurdistan are far removed from the logistical possibility of developing competitive professional careers. The current structure of Kurdish society is thus not conducive to the liberation of women. To begin moving in that direction, the region needs a large scale revision of the cultural values that repress women and check the advance of Kurdish society. This can only begin with the end of the patriarch, which will come when local people challenge the myth of men as superior and authoritative.

Similarly, the local idea of marriage is in dire need of reform. Marriage is a partnership between two people, based on an equal balance of power, even if tasks are distributed according to skill. Healthy partnerships are sustained by the guiding principles of respect, trust, friendship, honesty, loyalty and kindness—several of which seem absent or lopsided in some local marriages. That said, we cannot deny the existence of Kurdish marriages that honour equality and thrive on humane principles. It just so happens that the many I have observed function on a severely skewed value of power, whereby men make all decisions and women blindly obey. The institution of marriage needs work in the Kurdish region, but it is even more pressing that people stop indoctrinating girls to believe that marriage is their most important and ultimate goal in life.

Personally I do not oppose marriage. I support the union of two consenting adults who care for each other and nurture a healthy relationship. What I find unfair is a system that encases men in the role of income providers and turns women into domestic workers. Furthermore, as patriarchs, men are required to make all decisions affecting the family - a tradition that overwhelms them with psychological responsibility and wastes women's intellectual capacities. So why are men and women not challenging this dysfunctional system? Because some honour it as culture — again with culture as the almighty guard of patriarchy. The troubling part is that even women holding university degrees stand for culture as the legitimating force of backward custom. Take the extreme case of Dr Attia Saeed, a respected gynaecologist in the region; although highly educated and knowledgeable, Dr Saeed is known to address her patients in a brusk and demeaning manner. She once had a television program, in which she casually refers to women as "ignorant fools" and "stupid." Dr Saeed may feel frustrated with her patients' lack of information, but this should motivate her all the more to be kind and gentle in her efforts to educate women. Dr Saeed used abusive language to discuss issues affecting women, and she does so in a region where people have grown to accept abuse from authority. Since people admire Dr Saeed because of her education and experience, her behaviour vindicates and encourages the ill treatment of women. It also makes women uncomfortable about asking important questions about their health.

Women like Dr Saeed, who are in a position to influence society, have the power to teach men and women about healthy, empowering communication. Ideally this would be the preferred approach of such women, alas it is rarely the case in Kurdistan. Meanwhile in impoverished villages there are thousands of women who need to learn about contraception to manage reproduction more efficiently. Ignorance has caused many of them to induce abortions without medical help in desperate attempts to curtail the number of children in their families. Dr Saeed is aware of this tragic reality among poor women, but she still addresses them with inhumanity. How can people learn if an expert responds to them with antipathy and intolerance?

Kurdistan has many social problems, and we can change that by motivating young girls to think about the world and to encourage them in participating in activities that explore the world. Their ambitions should not be premised on marriage, love and romance (unless, that's their autonomous conclusion in life). Instead, they should be able to fully explore the possibilities and opportunities available to them.

We may nurture this journey by promoting philanthropy, voluntarism and discussions, particularly in schools, where young people spend a considerable part of their time learning. Action and organisation begin with exposure and communication, thus any viable long term change in society must follow a continuous period of education that stimulates young people to think freely and compassionately. The consistent implementation of such requires the commitment of human and financial resources and this is where government investment is crucial. While these progressive efforts are essential in the development of any society, they do not guarantee the formation of good character. However, they significantly increase the odds that people with great potential will receive an uncensored education on their way to adulthood and knowledge is the fundamental pillar of civilisation.

MEN OF RELIGION

"I love you when you bow in your mosque, kneel in your temple, pray in your church. For you and I are sons of one religion, and it is the spirit."

Khalil Gibran

Men dominate religious discourse in Kurdistan. People accept their interpretations, often reminiscent of prevalent views in neighbouring Arab countries, as unquestionable and sovereign. In mosques one sees imams present, but no female scholars. Even if there were female theologians in the region, they would have difficulty finding a job since the imams would not want to share their function with women. Thus imams interpret Islamic texts as they will and exclude women entirely from the opportunity to engage in the scholarly exploration of religion. In the rare instances when imams include women in discussions, they use gender as a point of attack to (falsely) illustrate that women lack the logical capacity to comprehend the Koran. This form of discrimination causes psychological and social damage to women. It is an incremental assault on their self-esteem and contributes to a culture of patriarchy that indoctrinates men and women to believe that femaleness comes with lower intellectual potential. But the functionality of patriarchy owes its success to mass compliance and obedience from women. When we sit on the margins of society nodding to authoritarian figures who insist on our inferiority, we approve our own subjugation. Of course many women stand idle because they depend on men to survive. Herein we find the vicious cycle of patriarchy: To make autonomous decisions women need financial stability to manoeuvre, but in Kurdistan many rely wholly on spousal support. This inherent problem reminds us that only education can assure complete independence for girls when they reach adulthood. The problem of women's social delay in Kurdistan is multidimensional and because they influence society so greatly, the clergy could play a significantly positive role in improving conditions for women. For this reason we must find ways to open discussion with imams and recruit their help in teaching people that women and men are beings born with equal potential for leadership.

People blame religion for much of women's delayed progress in Kurdistan; but religion itself is not the culprit of the ills of human society. For a very long time people have pointed the finger at Islam, for example, to justify women's oppression in the Middle East; but we forget that it is the way human beings conceptualise an idea that sets a precedence for the expression of values — and how these in turn manifest in the homes of people.

People misconstrue religion to incite shame and prevent women from expressing themselves. For example, many have cited religion to claim that women who walk alone in the evening or converse with unrelated men, are amoral and dishonourable. Hence, from a subjective interpretation of religion comes a corrupt value that manifests in society as a cultural stereotype. With great power the negative stereotype grows to be accepted as a universal truth that delineates the morality of women. The labyrinthine nature of this stereotype is especially dangerous because it is embedded in personality. We are inevitably the product of our societies, and when we grow hearing the same stories and statements, we integrate their value in the fabric of personal identity. To begin to address the problem properly, we must enlist the support of clerics to promote a positive image of women, along with their scholarly participation in religious education. The latter may take the form of women offering viewpoints different from the widely accepted interpretations of sacred scripture, which currently place women in a position inferior to men.

With all things considered, the fact remains that few Kurdish women make an effort to participate in religious meetings, where they may share new perspectives to counteract repressive notions of women's behaviour. One of the reasons for this may lie in the public perception that a woman interested in the study of religion is not attractive. Men in Kurdistan admire women who are modest, cultured and gentle. They prefer women who contain their rebellious streak on the surface and never use it to defy authority. Such image of women is one of contradiction, and it is common in Erbil, where most men run from the idea of women having an intellectual discussion about religion. The situation is unfortunate because it distances talented women from clerical circles and lessens their opportunity to influence imams. A case in point is that of women who have memorised the Koran, an astonishing feat, but never engage in debate or propose alternative, contemporary interpretations of the sacred text. Their silence is a disservice because these are the women in the best position to engage people in thought and show that negative beliefs concerning women are vastly unrelated to the wisdom put forth in the holy Koran.

The news is not all bad; there is at least one Kurdish province where outspoken women exist and routinely challenge reactionary ideas passed as religion. Women in Silemani are more involved in discussing Islam, Christianity, Buddhism, Judaism, Hinduism and other faiths, with little reticence or concern for how others may perceive the activity. It is puzzling that Erbil, often considered one of the more advanced provinces of the region, has fewer outspoken women than Slemani.

On Fridays families attend religious sermons throughout Kurdistan to honour their faith. As advised by the government, these services are rarely political and mostly spiritual. On such days, local women could seize the opportunity to discuss how the interpretation of faith affects social customs. Discussions of this nature would enrich their lives with the important intellectual component missing from daily routine. Their active participation in the discussion of religion would stimulate them to think critically about the flawed theories people accept as guidelines for women's behaviour. Like men, when women engage in the regular discussion of ideas, they improve their ability to reason and present arguments in a logical and respectable manner. Such activity would certainly benefit women in Erbil, where many chauvinistic practices originate in false representations of religion.

Although not always appreciated by writers and academics, Islam is a particularly significant religion in Kurdistan. This has been the case in the region for many centuries, as evidenced by its vast number of Kurdish Muslims. How did such a prized religion come to accommodate meaning that puts women at a disadvantage? The answer must come from its foremost representatives — clerics. Islam is an uncomplicated religion; its holy text — the Koran - outlines truths in a form that allows ample interpretation. Ironically, it is the Koran's inherently free structure that clerics have used to distort teachings in a way that compromises women's freedom. Their misinterpretations are in conflict with feminism, but such diversion does not come from Islam itself. Misinformed about the true significance of feminism and Islamic teachings, some people have come to perceive feminism as a wicked attempt to destroy religion. In truth, however, feminism does not exist to oppose religion, but to combat gender discrimination and establish equal rights for the people of a society. Naturally this effort requires a reevaluation of the ideals that oppress women.

When feminists identify oppressive dogma in the way people interpret and follow religion, they try to present an unbiased view of women, free from religious distortion. The honest, liberating nature of feminism requires this type of assessment. Thus the fight for gender equality invariably demands that people challenge certain religious theories. This does not mean that feminists should focus solely on criticising religion and blaming it for the global oppression of women. On the contrary, the investigative process should inspire an objective study and revision of ideas that structure society and guide human behaviour. That said, to dismantle patriarchy we must first recognise its religious threads. Some feminists ignore this relationship, others use the connection to inspire support for the feminist cause. The central theme of feminist ideology upholds a world where people of male and female genders enjoy equal opportunities in society. This core philosophy shows that the feminist cause is not a narrow fight against Islam or Christianity; it is more complex than that, and requires feminists to transcend the blame game and focus on the bigger picture. Since 2001, when criminals claiming to be true Muslims attacked the United States and killed thousands, Western feminism has been fixated on a criticism of Islam. For all its good intentions, the subsequent War on Terror left a deadly imprint in the feminist consciousness: People worldwide began to view Islam as the archenemy of women. More than one decade following the US tragedy we find ourselves in a dead end of distrust: people regard Islam as a religion that abuses women; and Muslims perceive feminists as amoral crusaders of Western civilisation. The general distrust has curbed the expansion of feminism. In Kurdistan, for example, feminism as an organised movement remains in its early stages. Local women have only now begun to explore the concept and the idea of establishing a group to challenge government policies and organisational structures that ignore women's rights.

BUREAUCRACY IN KURDISTAN

"Bureaucracy, the rule of no one, has become the modern form of despotism."

Mary McCarthy

During my recent time in Kurdistan I encountered a hefty bureaucratic system that demands permits for nearly every humanitarian activity. Our plans to visit inmates in prison nearly collapsed, as local institutions required our group to contact various authorities for official permission. During this process we had to explain repeatedly our reasons for visiting the prisoners, and declare how we intended to use information gathered at the facilities. The experience left some volunteers with the impression that the local government has an overly controlling approach toward its people, and this is unwise because it saturates people with anger — a key ingredient for revolution. I understand that leadership can never be perfect, particularly in a developing region like Southern Kurdistan. However, there are degrees of common sense, and I have learned — in my attempts to raise money for local orphans that reason is not guiding charitable efforts. The lack of timely cooperation from officials forces volunteers to knock on doors for minimal support. At the time of writing this, my group still awaits a permit to position fundraising booths in main cities and near malls. Every day gone is a day of opportunity lost, because booths can capture people's attention quickly, raise awareness about a cause and galvanise mass support in a nonintrusive way. The long delay in processing our permit has made some of us wonder if local authorities misunderstand our intentions. Our aim is to help poor, abandoned children in Kurdistan—we have no interest in inciting uncivilised behaviour of any sort. Could the heavy bureaucracy mean that local officials fear a rebellion, because they lead a disparate economy on ground fertile to revolt against the social ills that plague our nation.

This would help explain the tight control of humanitarian activities, which by definition expose troubling conditions, such as those found in local orphanages, where one sees the neglected side of development. In 2011 several countries experienced civil unrest ignited by long term oppression. The events in Tunisia, Egypt, Libya, Yemen, Bahrain and Syria remind us that human beings have a finite tolerance for indignity, a boiling point for suffering and injustice, if you will. From the Arab Spring we learn that when the ability to withstand abuse expires, a revolution explodes. Erbil — the pearl city of Kurdistan is still far from this point, but some regional areas have begun to witness the seeds of unrest. Erbil is where the Kurdistan Regional Government has its headquarters. It is also the city of my childhood, as shared earlier. I know the roads, the streets and the people who grow impatient under the shadow of inequality. Daily poverty gnaws their patience and substitutes calm with resentment. The working people of Kurdistan grow tired and in their fatigue rises the will to fight for a better quality of life. They struggle to survive each day, but the benefits of progress grow far in the distance. While regular shops sell drinks for one dollar, the modern cafes of air conditioned malls sell them for US$10, a price beyond the means of average people to consume on a daily basis, and reflective of a growing class division in Kurdistan.

Locally people handle time differently. When asked for public permits, civil servants tend to promise readily and deliver late. In some cases they keep applicants waiting in anxious anticipation only to inform them later that a "delicate government situation" forced officials to reject their application. This delicacy seems more like a period of open bribery than anything concretely sensitive. As people who support human rights and justice, how can we consider offering a bribe to move forward in our humanitarian work? Such bureaucratic nuances place us in a position of moral polarities, where wrong appears as temptation to facilitate good. Nevertheless we refuse to bow to corruption and accept the reality that our path to help people is fraught with obstacles.

Kurdish politics exist on a plane not meant for women and young people. It is an exclusive arena of older men who have accumulated experience of a less orthodox nature. These patriarchs have maintained a system that subsides on public labour in favour of a small, privileged elite. The absence of organised activism has allowed this perverse system to prevail for too long. Although many people recognise that there is room for significant improvement in local politics, they avoid taking action because they fear retaliation. Local officials are part of a governing body that oversees military and police forces, all of whom the public distrusts when it comes to disbanding corruption at the higher level. Young people, in particular, are protective of their lives and do not feel motivated to risk it in defence of honourable politics.

Women's ability to participate in politics or in activity to reform politics is severely limited, as discussed earlier. Those educated, who receive support from their families to study at university, also find themselves engulfed in a whirlwind of familial restrictions that leave little time and space for political activism. Some manage to expose issues anonymously via social media applications, but their efforts move at the speed of rudimentary internet connections. Faster bandwidth is costly in

Kurdistan and typically used by those 'better off', corporate offices and government entities. Still, despite the social and logistical odds against them, some women have turned online activism into a round-the-clock job. Safely hidden behind anonymous avatars, these women are breaking old rules and raising the voice of a new generation ready for change that defies injustice and honours equality.

Words alone are frivolous on Kurdish soil. The power of speech does not impress local folk, who have long yearned for action that can create tangible results and improve their daily circumstances. However, people wait for change to occur without their help. Thus when young volunteers try to ameliorate conditions for the poor, and government workers create unnecessary barriers, they withhold support that could manifest as a wise investment in the advancement of their communities.

I know not which government office exercises the most authority over community affairs and charitable foundations, but my experience of running in circles to attain a permit for an information booth has taught me that local management is plagued with deficiencies. Government employees of all levels seem to lack a linear schedule of laws that enforces consistency and legal manoeuvring in the handling of public requests. As matters stand, one is tempted to believe that personal preference may guide official decisions that affect a multitude of factors, including permits to educate people about poverty in Kurdistan. Such inconsistencies are the consequences of corruption at work and deceit serves only to feed exploitation and squash progress.

LOVE

"True love is not a strong, fiery, impetuous passion. It is, on the contrary, an element calm and deep. It looks beyond mere externals, and is attracted by qualities alone. It is wise and discriminating, and its devotion is real and abiding."

Ellen G. White

When I visited private homes in Gilkend — one of the poorest areas of Erbil province —   I met an elderly couple coping with particularly challenging circumstances. They lived alone in a diminutive home, where they endured the excruciating heat of summer. On the day of my visit — as on many other days —   there was no electricity and the high temperature left perpetual beads of sweat on the gentleman's forehead. The air was stifling. The man and the woman had no children, and neither of them could read or write. The two struggled daily to provide for themselves, an effort facilitated by the kindness of neighbours who shared goods with them on a regular basis. Gentle and proud, the couple preferred not to seek favours but expressed much gratitude for the generosity of others — without which the very essence of their lives would be at risk. It was their story of survival that took me to a child nearby.

Eleven-year-old Bayan Ali had sat motionless on the front steps of a house nearby watching me engage the neighbourhood residents in conversation. Her hands were empty but she kept her gaze intently focused on my activity. After meeting a few families and hearing their stories, I approached Bayan with a smile. As customarily done in the region, I referenced the weather and asked why she was not at home. "We have no electricity and the generators are off. It's very hot inside, but it's just as hot outside!" The end of her sentence came with laughter and she conceded that the air was more tolerable outdoors. We continued chatting, as I joined her on the steps. I was happy to learn that she still attended school, an achievement not always possible for those from extremely poor backgrounds. Bayan's insights about her educational experience illustrated the challenges facing local families: "No one likes to go to school feeling poor or less than others there." As she spoke, Bayan's hazel eyes accompanied the movements of my pen, as if to help form the letters on my notepad. I could see that she was a thoughtful child keenly interested in the power of words.

"Ruwayda, are you still in school?" the young girl asked. When I told her that I had finished studying, she wanted to know the name of my school. Kingston University in England had been the last one, I said, noticing an immediate transformation on Bayan's face. Her smile widened and she leaned toward me with lively anticipation, as she assumed the role of spontaneous interviewer. My university days flashed before me and I saw images of classmates enthralled in wasteful debauchery. I remembered how disappointed I had felt to see them explore pubs instead of London's intellectual life. I withheld this less appealing facet of young adulthood to avoid corrupting the enthusiasm of a child, for whom the world's possibilities are filled with benevolence. I looked at Bayan firmly and put all my effort in conveying that if she studied everyday and earned good grades, she could one day apply for a scholarship to study in Europe. I focused on the positive aspects of the experience, and told her that at university people live independently and meet others from all corners of the globe. There she would form meaningful friendships and gain knowledge about world customs, history and systems — all of which would forever enlighten her life with purpose. She would walk the streets in total liberty, deciding in which direction to go, free from the limitations of Gilkend. Bayan now sat wide eyed, her face filled with wonder and eager determination. In that moment I knew the importance of nurturing a child's imagination with the possibility of a bright future. I understood that in these small acts we present a blueprint from which children arrange the building blocks of their future. In Bayan's questions I saw the outline of a prosperous Kurdistan, where people from all walks of life can access education to live productively and safe from poverty.

Despite her young age, Bayan was insightful and able to express her thoughts clearly. She was also observant and recognised the benefits of privilege missing from her life: "Rich kids have better notebooks, bags, clothes, shoes, phones, everything. They do well in school because their parents pay for tutors to help them with homework." Her comments illustrated the need for more government funding, which would allow schools to provide extra classes for students experiencing difficulties. Such approach would improve students' performance at school without adding financial burden to their parents. It would also strengthen their self-esteem, as they would not see modest resources as a determinant of poor grades.

Bayan came from a family of six children. When I spoke with her mother I learned that the family struggled financially and lived in poor conditions. The children, all enrolled in school, frequently needed supplies that Bayan's parents could not afford to buy. Although I did not ask, the mother confided that their generous number of children was the result of her husband's desire to have a son, which arrived only after five girls. She adored her children and this was undoubtedly clear — but said the cost of raising them was high and daunting. Her voice trembled with emotion and tears welled in her eyes as she spoke. I could see that this woman was a good mother stretching her resources beyond possibility to educate her children.

Although Kurdish culture has progressed positively in many ways, it retains certain values that fall short of progress. Among them is the idea that babies born male are more important than others. This backward notion is so pervasive that it pressures some families to reproduce until the arrival of a boy. For many the effort brings permanent financial woes that constrict the support of existing children. Still, awareness of this factor does not deter the quest for boy. The practice is troubling and reveals the categorical structure of human hierarchy in the region.

RABAR

"Your children are not your children. They are the sons and daughters of Life's longing for itself. They came through you but not from you and though they are with you yet they belong not to you."

Khalil Gibran

Like my parents before me, I was born in the city of Erbil. I arrived in the world on a cold November afternoon in 1989, many years after two brothers and a sister. I am told family and friends were delighted with the arrival of a new baby. As the story goes, mother went into labour while my father and oldest brother Rabar travelled through Koye, a Kurdish town near the province of Erbil. When they heard the news they rushed to Erbil to find a plump baby of voluminous cheeks slumbering peacefully in an incubator. My early years thereafter would see me somewhat incubated because of political turmoil in the region.

At that time my father's work required him to be in Slemani, while my mother remained with the children in Erbil in a modest home of two bedrooms. I can imagine that those were tough days for mother in particular, who was responsible for the daily care of four children. But father visited regularly and when he did the entire family was joyous. In 1990 the Gulf War erupted and we moved to Shaqlawe, a town to the northeast of Erbil. The ensuing period brought great tragedy, as my oldest brother Rabar fell ill and became an unwitting casualty of war when he could not reach a hospital.

It was a heart-wrenching time for my mother and father. It caused mother to withdraw in unbearable grief. Her body stiffened with the weight of despair and left her incapable of consuming nourishment for weeks. Life had surrendered her child to death, leaving the air too barren for her to breathe without a struggle. The abyss of sorrow did not spare father from desperation either. It engulfed him with equal might and paralysed his will to speak or move. Neither of my parents had been able to hold Rabar in death or attend his funeral. All around people had a difficult time believing that he had left our world. I was merely a toddler and all I remember of Rabar's passing are the sad details I learned from relatives. The photographs and stories of his life I treasure in my heart with pride and everlasting love.

Twenty-one years have passed since Rabar died, but his friends keep his memory alive and speak fondly of him. Their stories reveal that he was inclined toward justice, as evidenced in his treatment of girls, whom he defended against brutality when few men in Kurdistan challenged the inherent barbarity of physical violence. Recently I heard that once, when a cousin of ours struck a girl and left her visibly bruised, Rabar located her and asked her to describe the attack in detail — in front of our cousin. On hearing his victim relate the ordeal to Rabar, our cousin felt shame and understood that it is the absence of manhood that compels a man to strike a woman, not the other way round. Rabar was also thoughtful and generous, even in times of strife. During the Gulf War, when access to goods became unstable and illness had already seized him, Rabar still managed to visit home with a bag of apples, which he knew were his baby sister's favourite fruit. Mother would take one in her hand and use a spoon to scrape the inner, juicy parts for me. My early childhood is filled with such stories, rich in simplicity and utter joy, but it is also marked by contrasting moments of sheer desperation, when I felt the imminent threat of violent death. Sadly my generation was not the last to grow up amid violence in Kurdistan. Intolerance and inhumanity from neighbouring states continue to torment the Kurdish people. In most parts of greater Kurdistan, the conflict refuses to wane and the suffering never stops. Southern Kurdistan is the one exception, where Kurdish people now have a genuine chance to live free of ethnic cleansing. Despite these small steps, the geographical spread of greater Kurdistan, which encompasses parts of Iran, Iraq, Syria and Turkey has made it difficult for Kurds to establish unity. The absence of a unified presence makes the Kurdish position more vulnerable in the region. Antagonists continually use this disadvantage to impose political and territorial sanctions on Kurds, violate their human rights, and demand their assimilation into other cultures.

For decades the Iraqi Baath party controlled Southern Kurdistan. During that period the people endured civil war, extreme poverty and ongoing humiliation at the hands of men who measured humanity in degrees of ethnicity. Although the Iraqi Kurds were freed from the regime in 2003 when the US invaded, they never fully recovered from the effects of prolonged abuse. The scars left by inhumane treatment are far deeper than the marks of torture; they run deep in the human psyche, where they pollute every thought, memory or idea. This post traumatic phenomenon forms a permanent state of passivity gilded by fright that, like the horrific effects of nuclear disasters, remains in the social consciousness of a region for several generations. We can see the manifestation of this unfortunate chain of events in Southern Kurdistan, where people are reluctant to oppose social injustice because they fear punishment. The situation is compounded by the fact that Kurds have long endured deadly conflict among their own religious and political groups.

My childhood is filled with memories of war and political activities. From a small radio I often heard patriotic songs and the names of prominent politicians. The radio had been a gift from my father, who also gave one to my girlfriends on our street. Most of us were around seven years old at the time. We would sit together and marvel at the sound coming from the small black boxes. It was around this time that politics began to shape our beliefs in various directions. Some of us watched our parents grow convinced that Kurdish people should enjoy life free from strict government control. Undoubtedly this progressive environment contained its own flavour of (positive) indoctrination. Thus my little friends and I grew to believe in the causes our parents supported in much the same way a young boy in England might develop an affinity toward the football team his father follows.

From 1994 to 1997 Kurdistan was the stage of a deadly conflict between two political parties: the

Kurdistan Democratic Party and the Patriotic Union of Kurdistan. This civil war claimed thousands of lives and wrecked havoc on all aspects of local development. From this period one particularly harrowing night still haunts me. I experience it as a recurring nightmare that blurs the line between sleep and wakefulness, somehow establishing a permanent reality suspended in time. It happened on a cold winter night when our family travelled by car through Rewanduz, a town in the northeast of Iraqi Kurdistan. My brother Rebaz sat in the front passenger seat while my father drove. Mother was in the back with my sister Ronahe and me. A small bag packed hastily with family heirlooms, emergency money and passports rested on her lap. She kept her hands closed tightly around Ronahe's and mine, which grew clammy, as my heart raced. Suddenly several vehicles surrounded our car and men wielding machine guns ordered us to stop. In the rearview mirror my father's eyes turned to ice, his skin hardened like stone and he accelerated. My mother's grip tightened around our hands. Inside we remained silent as cars and a Jeep blocked our path on all sides. "Please let my wife and children go!

Take me!" my father's voice pierced the dense air like a bullet. On cue my mother reached for the door next to Ronahe and opened it wide, quickly ushering us onto the hardened floor. Cold wind pressed my cheeks. A dog barked in the distance. I imagined his teeth sharp and his mouth large with thick drops of saliva cascading to the ground. "Run! Run to the houses!" urged mother, her voice breaking with an odd mix of despair and certainty. Ronahe took my hand into hers and ran fast, my small arm becoming an extension of hers. Mother's voice faded in the background.

We ran until we reached the houses lining the street beyond the road. We threw our open palms on an endless succession of doors. A sinister light hovered above our chilling cries. Tears began to form an icy stream on my face. "Please open the door! Please help us!" Ronahe and I pleaded as we banged with urgency. Finally a door opened slightly to reveal the face of a woman. "Go away, leave, go!" she said. Her eyes widened and squinted under a knitted brow marked by imposing lines bathed in the night sky. Her disinterest forced our panic into momentary paralysis. We felt numbed by the terrifying possibility that our family lay dead on the road. The low temperature pricked our fingers with invisible needles. Our hands swelled from hammering on doors. I was not yet eight years of age on the night fate introduced me to terror and inhumanity; but I was old enough to learn that kindness follows choice.

As we walked back to the road, we remembered that Rebaz had discarded our father's pistol when the militias surrounded our car. During the civil war many people carried guns for their protection, but opponents cited this as evidence of planned attack. Thus any possibility of father's survival depended on the successful concealment of his weapon. The thought gave us hope of finding him alive. We continue walking until we spotted our mother standing motionless on the road, her face buried in her hands. Father and Rebaz had been taken, along with the car and our few possessions. Fear enveloped me as wails punctuated mother's breathless sobs.

My tongue became metal and a giant clamp sealed my lungs. Unseen chains weighing tonnes encircled my feet until Ronahe squeezed my arm to animate my body. We ran to mother and fell into her arms in a chorus of anguish, as people watched from their homes. The memory of this day stops here, but I am told that someone who knew my mother arranged for our return to Slemani. We would later reunite with father and Rebaz, who had both been released unscathed. The Kurdish civil war ended soon after.

My childhood memories are coloured with images of loss and death, but amidst them I find joyous moments spent with family and friends. Despite their traumatic marks, the varied experiences of my past have taught me valuable lessons and enriched my life with perspective. I realise that the Kurdish civil war still influences my perception of the world and the decisions I make, so I wonder about its adverse effects on a generation of children brought up during that period. I imagine that they are profound and residual, and have a substantial impact on identity and behaviour. The lack of literature on the subject should inspire the regional government to investigate the effects of war on children. Psychologists have long documented the psychological injuries observed in survivors of war, so we must recognise them in children, whose vulnerability and dependence places them at particular risk in conflict zones. When we acknowledge the trauma of young survivors, we can begin to understand how their experience of war motivates them in adulthood, and how this cause and effect contributes to shaping societies.

My parents made a wise choice when they relocated our family to England in 2000. London provided a multicultural context with ample opportunity for the boundless exploration of identity. Through my experience as a young newcomer, I came to assimilate in a culture that felt safe. This assimilation process — which I chose — has comforted me with a dual identity that allows me to see the world through a lens unencumbered by the restrictions of exclusive patriotism. As a British Kurdish person I can appreciate the best traditions of two very different cultures and integrate their positive aspects in my life. My inclination toward Britain began when the country welcomed our family and provided shelter and education to support our integration. Soon after leaving Kurdistan, we were enrolled in classes to teach us to speak English fluently. As our vocabulary grew, the ground beneath our feet felt more solid, and we slowly built confidence in our new home. Throughout the transition period mother and father continued to share knowledge about Kurdish culture. Their efforts manifested in perfect measure because today my sense of self embodies the amalgamation of British and Kurdish cultures.

Nevertheless the initial years in the UK were not free from culture shock. We had left an environment sustained by patriarchal structure, where the will of men dictated the fate of women. Now we found ourselves in a society that honoured the legal premise of gender equality. In England people seemed to enjoy a sense of individuality removed from the obligatory focus of family and community alliances. It was markedly different from Kurdistan, where the latter practices moulded society. Father's liberal outlook helped him adapt readily to this change, but mother — who has more conservative tendencies — struggled to adapt in the early days. Ronahe and I, benefiting from the malleability of youth, plunged headfirst into our new world. Our initial inability to communicate in English did not deter our curiosity, but it did contribute to my quiet and perceptually odd demeanour at school. Many times I used Kurdish to address classmates, a behaviour that accentuated our differences. I recall in particular an incident in the sixth grade when mother had given me a bag of sweets. This was no ordinary gift, so I kept the sweets in my schoolbag and began to eat them at the playground during recess. On seeing this, one girl approached me and said something, pointing to the sweets. I perceived this as her attempt to say that students were not allowed to eat on the playground, so I ran to a corner in panicked silence and consumed the entire bag with ferocious speed. In retrospect I realise that my classmate may have been asking for one of my prized treats, but I do not know for sure whether she meant to warn or savour and I remain curious.

Apart from occasional misinterpretations, my primary school experience in exile was unremarkable. Teachers were kind and helpful, and promoted drawing and painting activities, which I enjoyed thoroughly, given my appreciation for the arts. Other classes received less of my participation, but this was a consequence of the barrier standing between English and Kurdish. Still, I can remember teachers cautioning students to not sniff glue — I complied eagerly (a random memory that popped into my head).

By the time I reached seventh grade I could communicate confidently in English. Many still perceived me as a newcomer and I felt this myself, but I got by without major philosophical crises or premature assessments of identity. This would change in eighth grade — the year I began to question the relevance of religion. As a student at a Catholic school for girls, I soon felt that obligatory church attendance was not quite right for me. Although I appreciated their melody and devotion, I felt disconnected from the biblical hymns the school required all students to memorise. Affected by these feelings, I challenged a teacher and tried to make the case for why the school should not impose religious service and gospel verses on people from Islamic traditions. The teacher responded promptly with detention and orders to copy the Hail Mary prayer a dozen times. I concealed the exchange from my parents, but in hindsight I wish I had told them, as their insight would have satisfied my need for objective debate. Amusingly, I see now that the episode at school was my first legal battle. I lost the case, but triumphed in challenging a fundamentally unjust practice.

My daring feat, however, did not alter the school policy — given that it was a Catholic institution and thus service was integral to its curriculum at the time — so I continued to attend church regularly with my classmates. Most of the girls found the solemn occasion rather amusing — as young people often do — and were plagued by persistent giggles throughout the priestly worship. Religious significance of the event usually fell at the mercy of youthful abandon, no matter how devout the student. The behaviour was disrespectful, particularly when we convulsed drinking Ribena as a wine substitute for the blood of Christ. Alas, early adolescence is characterised by uncontrollable goofiness that targets situations requiring seriousness. Thus we sat in rows chattering, giggling and passing notes before the holy pulpit. The teachers observed this from the aisles under pronounced frowns, often approaching the offending rows with reprimands and the promise of more homework and detention. Unfortunately their efforts to enforce discipline were futile, and eventually they relented and reduced our church days to special occasions, such as Easter and Christmas. The church remained open year-round, and a pipe organ continued to fill its atrium with ethereal sounds interspersed by the dreadful chants of student choirs.

The middle school years were a lesson in culture, during which I learned about the diverse people of Britain and their customs. Throughout this time my parents' main concern was the quality of my grades, which I maintained relatively 'good' to their satisfaction, even if my interest was not always genuine. For instance, while completing science assignments I regularly copied information from the required book to answer questions. The teachers supported this method, but I found it disingenuous since it did not encourage original investigation or thought. On the other hand, English literature demanded more cognitive autonomy and stimulated my imagination to run free. I remember when the class read Of Mice and Men. John Steinbeck's novel about the tribulations of two migrant workers in California during the 1930s. I was moved equally by prose and plot, and I believe the book had a profound impact on how I came to appreciate eloquence in language.

The adjustment years in England were marked by our parents' efforts to instil Kurdish identity in their children. This included the daily integration of Kurdish etiquette and cuisine in our lifestyle. We watched middle eastern television, celebrated Kurdish holidays and enjoyed a solid network of Kurdish friends throughout London. London is a vibrant city where anyone belongs because its people come from various ethnic and social groups. The presence of so many cultures, some infused together, enriches British society and allows people to embrace a local identity that does not displace primary heritage.

Full adolescence arrived in this scenario of endless opportunity and so I explored without trepidation. Each phase — Goth, punk, chic — shook my poor parents with equal perplexity and dread. Throughout each I knew that my exploration was only temporary as I searched for an image that harmonised with my inner identity. I noticed then that many of my friends had been raised to appreciate particular genres of music, but I felt like an open vessel to rhythm. I wanted to listen to anything and everything, with total disregard for constrictions of cool. It was this attitude (and my parents' progressive patience) that allowed me to turn full circle and meet Kurdish culture on my own terms. I began to explore Islam with the same objectivity I had questioned Christianity. Apart from basic teachings received from my parents, I had little knowledge of Islam. I turned to libraries and embarked on a scholarly exploration that still guides me today.

I began with Islam, the book by Karen Armstrong, which takes readers on a journey from the sixth century forward, detailing significant events in the history of Islam. When I finished reading it I wanted to learn more about the beliefs that guide human societies, so I continued to seek material about Islam and other predominant religions, as well as atheism — their antithetical philosophy. Ironically, the first phase of my research journey came to an end when I entered college, which consumed most of my time with rudimentary assignments. Sometimes students generated debate, but I found the intellectual component lacking. Mostly my classmates seemed occupied with drinking, clubbing and dating — all activities that did not spark my interest. There was one exception, however — a fellow student, equally bored by such affairs, who challenged me in fervent discussions. Ifrah and I would develop a close friendship. We were naive then, but sensible enough to read books on political theory so we could unnerve our Government and Politics instructor, whom we perceived to harbour an imperialistic view of the Middle East. We struggled to understand his arguments and find academically cohesive responses to challenge the way he exposed political dialectic. Our quest to learn — if only to counteract his stance — stands as proof that the man was an excellent teacher. This was further evidenced by the fact that Ifrah and I spent considerable time discussing politics outside the classroom.

Our awareness of mounting global turmoil in

the new millennium pressed our urge to learn. We felt a certain responsibility for the world, as wars raged in Africa and the Middle East, creating humanitarian crises in civilian populations. We understood that in some cases foreign governments wage war as the ultimate attempt to restore regional civility and implement a viable political structure that does not oppress people. Our realisation of this pained us on a human level, but it was clear that in some instances only warfare can restore peace. Ifrah and I met often in London's coffee shops to discuss such world affairs before we attended class. We enjoyed participating in debates, and felt a rising need to remain intellectually engaged in matters of political consequence. When we watched the Lost Boys of Sudan, a documentary film about the extraordinary struggle of orphaned children in war-torn Africa, we learned that conflict comes in many layers, some of them intolerably disgraceful. The film had been recommended to us by the same instructor whose views we challenged habitually. Mr Martin had suggested the film after noting that Ifrah and I entertained a narrow view of the Middle East and needed to cultivate a broader understanding of reality. He was right, of course, and I cherish his honesty and patience, without which our learning would have been compromised.

I enrolled at Kingston Law School in the fall of 2009, soon after completing college. My time as a university student would take me through a long, demanding journey that turned my views in every possible and unexpected direction. Before then I had treasured a linear attachment to the spiritual guidance of Islam, which had provided solace, peace and love throughout my life. Now I encountered feminism — an ideology that upholds gender equality in all sectors of society. I read first the works of Steinem and Beauvoir, widely considered essential feminist literature, and learned to identify ideas that harboured repressive ideologies about women. The knowledge motivated me to challenge oppressive notions that hinder women's advancement in the world. My commitment earned me the reputation of troublemaker among religious groups on campus. They disliked my efforts to inspire an examination of beliefs that belittle women or minimise their potential to achieve. The position was not pleasant, but I could not allow emotions to distract me from the moral obligation of discrediting bigotry. As a developing feminist in a sometimes hostile environment, I discovered an enlightening link between feminism and the fundamental teachings of Islam: the belief that all people are created equal. This realisation accentuated my spiritual connection to Islam and showed me that as a Muslim I could draw on the strengths of feminism to promote justice. Through my frequent discussions with people — many of them opposing my arguments — I learned to debate viewpoints from multiple angles. I became vice president of the debating society on campus during my first year at university and served as president the year after. Throughout this time I researched the goals of various political and humanitarian organisations, so by the third year of my studies I felt ready to participate in real world activism. I joined a network of international activists and journalists, from whom I received guidance and information concerning historical events. It was through them that I came to broaden my understanding of the Middle East within a geopolitical context.

I left Southern Kurdistan as a child, but returned regularly thereafter to spend summers with relatives and friends. In 2012, intending to conduct research, I based my stay in our family home in Erbil. This allowed me to organise several visits to impoverished villages, where I could interview people. Their stories present a fuller picture of the Kurdistan of today, one in which educational opportunity and economic privilege draw a class line between prosperity and poverty.

Nevertheless if we compare Southern Kurdistan with Iraq's Arab enclaves, we see that Iraqis are burdened by more severe conditions: limited electricity averaging six hours per day; frequent suicide bombings; extreme gender restrictions; and rampant corruption in government. Despite foreign intervention since the 1960s, Iraq continues to lack a system of accountability capable of supporting justice. People do not know political stability, and spend most of their time trying to survive in a defective system that cannot protect their human rights. But even comparatively, Kurdistan is not the judicial haven or rising utopia portrayed in some media narratives. The truth is the region has areas where people live in abject poverty that forces children to replace school with exploitative labour, and where prisons are battered women's only refuge. I understand that some writers choose to project a positive image of Kurdistan, but this should not interfere with the ability to present an unbiased picture. Rosy pictures are great for children's books, but do not help educate an adult public about the inadequacies of a developing region. Honesty supports progress and justice, and real patriotism does not require a biased view of the world. The other end of misrepresentation paints Kurdistan as hell on Earth, where man runs amok compelled by savagery, impossibly removed from the forces of civilisation. Surely reality in Kurdistan must fall somewhere between extreme constructs of the demonic and divine. Progress is being made in the region, but it is leaving many people behind and sowing the seeds of a class war. So how do we begin to address the problem of rising economic disparity in Kurdistan? With courage, humanity and objectivity we research the nature of the region's social problems and political frameworks. We make assessments and work with local leaders to implement structures that help poor and disadvantaged populations. We remember that social problems are similar to bacterial infections - they spread and kill in the absence of treatment.

MASTAW

"Thousands of tired, nerve-shaken, over-civilized people are beginning to find out that going to the mountains is going home; that wildness is a necessity."

John Muir

The mountains of Erbil province are now surrounded by new roads, houses and construction sites. The changed scenery is remarkable. In the early 1990s the area had few sustained roads, and most were unpaved, narrow, bumpy and prone to induce nausea. I recall many nauseating rides from Slemani to Erbil, when mother would try to comfort my siblings and me, as father drove attentively through the rough terrain. On such rides I usually rested my head on mother's lap under her gentle hand, or cried and whined incessantly to protest the hot, humid weather.

From a distance the first Erbil village looks unchanged. The roads leading to Kani Shwardi are mud pathways covered with dirt, and the ride is a steep sequence of bumps. When I arrive at the first house the owners greet me in Kurdish manner — hospitable and pleased — and invite me inside their home. They give me a cold drink, and it brings relief in the intense summer heat that turns my cheeks crimson. I share my plan to interview people and learn about life in the village. As the conversation progresses, the Hamdia Khan household fills with neighbours and relatives wanting to see the visitor who has come from afar.

Morning shone bright still when I left Hamdia's home, so I walked through the village and chatted with local people as they went about daily routines. Many were preoccupied with not being able to access medical care or schools, and most complained about the scarcity of farming water, as echoed earlier by Hamdia: "We can't farm in our village. We have to drive to other places to buy fruit and vegetables. What's the point of a village if people can't farm? How are we supposed to earn a living?" Hamdia had asked rhetorically with hands apart framing an expression of disbelief. The water shortage had created an unemployment crisis among the village men, who typically work the land. Now, Hamdia lamented, the men had no choice but to seek work in central cities. Their forced migration was creating a de facto separation among families, and decimating the cultural and organisational structures of village life.

The village people possessed neither drilling machines to dig wells nor hydraulic equipment to extract water from the ground. Financially it was impossible for them, or the local governing body, to acquire the machinery. Kani Shwardi had thus become progressively arid and forced unusual hardship upon its inhabitants. The problem was serious. I thought about places where luscious trees stand and fruit grows abundantly, and imagined how water would restore life in the village. I envisioned children playing under massive trees whose leaves embrace the sands of winds city bound.

My next stop was the nearby village of Baxche. I struggled on foot to reach the first house in sight. I reached the front door drenched in sweat with my feet caked in dust and dirt. I knocked, relieved with the promise of rest, but received no response. My journey to the area had been long — a lengthy drive followed by walking between the villages. I was fatigued, and disappointed to find no one in this home. I stood before the door momentarily and waited for someone to come. When reason set in, I walked across the street to a farmhouse surrounded by an enclosure housing chickens and goats. The animals stood on barren soil and appeared skeletal under the scorching summer sun. "Welcome!" shouted a voice from behind. The woman, advanced in age, wore traditional Kurdish clothing. Her hair was parted in the middle, each side plaited neatly. She invited me inside her home, where two women joined us with apologies for not having answered their door earlier. "We were napping", said one of them laughing. "We finished our chores, so we decided to nap for a bit", added the other, dispelling any impression of slothfulness. One of the women gave me a glassful of yoghurt juice, which I drank happily despite tasting slight acidity.

The women of Baxche were honest and comfortable discussing the challenges of local life. I mentioned domestic abuse and honour killings, and asked about the resources available to women fleeing violence. They returned laughter in response. Then one eyed me sombrely and declared: "Women here take what they get from their husbands." I understood that the village culture attributed absolute power to men in marriage contracts. Thus the villagers expected women to accept this premise from the moment they married, and whether bliss or brutality followed the deed was irrelevant. This was the norm in Baxche, and women who fell outside the mould experienced the wrath of correction.

I visited other villages in Erbil province and throughout them I identified three main concerns among people: Insufficient water to sustain farms; lack of access to medical care; and the unavailability of quality education for minors. While noting this on the drive to a sixth village, I noticed hives on my left arm — the unmistakable sign that I had consumed an excessive amount of yoghurt juice. Cultural etiquette (and thirst) had required that I accept all yoghurt drinks offered by the village residents. A rejection of their generous hospitality would have offended my hosts and projected an attitude of superiority from my part. Thus I had drunk several creamy juices, thanked the hosts profusely and praised the unique flavour of each drink, despite feeling increasingly nauseous.

Finally my body launched a protest. I became ill, away from a medical facility, and experienced a fraction of the fear that the villagers must feel in worse circumstances. The defining difference was that, unlike them, I had the option to return to Erbil city for medical attention. In the end a cold shower at home was enough to pacify the rash, and I had gained firsthand insight about village life.

Southern Kurdistan is breathtaking, but the beauty of the physical landscape is not what drew me in this direction. I traveled through the region to determine how people in comfortable positions can help improve living conditions for those less fortunate. I have a parallel interest in how traditional practices encase gender in social hierarchies and sustain a culture of patriarchy. Thus I have tried to understand how men and women think locally. What rules do they consider infallible? How do their values affect communal structures? Do local customs exist in a patriarchal framework that shapes personality? Understanding these complex relations required consistent observation that necessarily cascaded outside of fieldwork. Thus at social events I played the dual role of participant-observer, shifting discussions to the topic of women's emancipation, to engage people and observe their reactions. I saw that some men and women became agitated with the mention of feminism, and referred to the movement as "peculiar" or "irritating". By listening to the company I kept with the same care that I dedicated to the subjects of my interviews, I came to learn about the various dimensions of the Kurdish mindset.

Although frequently discussed in Kurdish circles, feminism carries a negative connotation in Kurdistan. People seem to regard feminists unfavourably because they feel uncomfortable with the idea of women's unlimited participation in society. So why is this happening? Many cultures present women as inferior to men — a representation that sets the course for restrictions that curtail women's freedom, development and participatory leadership. In this deficient social context, women who challenge the status quo are inevitably perceived as a nuisance or anomalous. A careful examination of patriarchal traditions in Kurdistan shows that the region must revise its understanding of women to acknowledge their full potential. Such a turn would introduce a new thread in the cultural milieu, and allow people to consider the social significance of feminism. It is from this angle that people would come to understand that feminism and Kurdish culture do not have to stand in opposition, but can form connected threads to move Kurdistan forward. And there is another construct in need of revision in the region and other parts of the world: The superman myth. The image of men as omnipotent and heroic protectors exists in contrast to women as weak and dependent. Thus the very ideology of feminism (which upholds equality among the sexes) stands against the superman myth. How can people raised to believe in the unfailing strength of men vis-à-vis the unending weakness of women turn to support feminism? To do so they must dismantle the false model of manhood that pressures men and degrades women — and such an enormous task requires lawful inspiration from governing institutions.

Patriarchal systems patronise and oppress women directly, but they thrive on the active participation of both genders. So how do women take part in this process? When they slander women who have successful careers, they discourage women from seeking opportunities that lead to financial independence. Their defamatory activity therefore strengthens an environment that distances women from the posts generally occupied by men. Women as such hold the dual role of perpetrators and victims in a culture of female subordination. Naivety also perpetuates patriarchy. For example, when privileged women claim to have achieved their goals because equal opportunity exists in Kurdistan, they promote fiction that stifles social change. The reality is that most successful women in the region have wealthy families who can transcend the roadblocks of patriarchy and pave their way toward success. This advantage does not discredit the women's hard work, but shows that their success is ensured by comfortable living conditions, prime access to education and influential connections. These privileges are the exclusive fortune of an elite minority. Thus when women of means misrepresent Kurdistan as a haven of equality, they popularise a myth that ignores the oppressive conditions keeping most women behind men. Although harm is not their intent, their actions are in effect an insidious reinforcement of patriarchy.

POVERTY

"In a country well governed, poverty is something to be ashamed of. In a country badly governed, wealth is something to be ashamed of."

Confucius

When children experience continuous deprivation they develop a handicapped perception of the world that compromises their understanding of possibility. Although hardship may motivate exceptional children to excel against the odds and escape poverty, for most it works as a pressure vacuum that leads to a life of servitude. The problem of neglected children is one typified in the orphanages of Kurdistan. There they live in miserable conditions, ignored by adult caretakers, and internalise the implicit message that they are worthless. This sense of wretchedness is particularly damaging because it cripples imagination and prevents children from envisioning a better future. Yet, quite remarkably, many of the orphanage children I met have retained passionate curiosity for the world outside. There is great hope in this, as it signals that proper intervention can help them recover from years of terrible penury to become healthy, happy and productive members of Kurdish society.

With the help of generous sponsors, who provided transportation, local volunteers and I tried to organise activities that offered stimulation to these children. One of the trips included a visit to Family Fun, a Erbil amusement park popular among families. Initially we had planned the trip for the older children in the orphanage, as they are more physically independent and require less assistance to move about. However, as we prepared to leave, it became clear that the younger residents needed to feel included, so we took everyone. As the buses departed, the children began to sing and clap, visibly delighted with the day ahead. We joined them singing the Kurdish anthem, and it was truly a happy ride for children and volunteers — until we arrived at Family Fun. There we learned that the park staff had not prepared the tickets for our group, so we had to wait in line for a prolonged time. Aya — a child who regularly asked me to adopt her — grew thirsty and impatient. She expressed her frustration with repeated requests for a milkshake, and inquiries about the park rides.

In between she offered defeated complaints of fatigue. Aya was vocal about her discontent, but she was not the only one feeling uneasy with the long wait. The older children had grown visibly uncomfortable waiting alongside the younger ones, so we separated them accordingly to give the teenagers more space to interact. This provided some relief and allowed us to supervise the younger children more closely.

Finally the doors opened to our group and we entered the park without hesitation. I was caught unprepared when two young children kissed my hands to express their gratitude for the adventure. The moment brought me to tears — I felt undeserving, weak, insignificant and distressed. Children should not feel obliged to express such gratefulness for an opportunity to enjoy their basic right to play and have fun. Their gentle act illustrated how little they thought of themselves — proof that society had failed them. I felt sick realising that we — the adults of Kurdish society — were responsible for this failure. I kissed their small hands in return and communicated gently that they were not required to kiss anyone's hands.

Kurdistan has many social problems, and poverty is one of the most pressing. Yet people who comprise the region's elite minority often believe that the poor feign poverty to beg and avoid work. The existence of this self-serving argument — based more on heartlessness than logic — is troubling. It favours a stereotype that blames poor people for their poverty and exonerates the rich for the dis- parity. In reality most people who beg on street corners are neither lazy nor deceitful, as implied by those who choose to ignore a growing public crisis. While the rich nurture disdain for the poor and ignore the hardships of the average Kurd, the regional government pays the difference in the form of food vouchers allotted to needy families. (Unfortunately this provision is indiscriminate and also benefits individuals for whom the aid is not essential.) These allowances may prevent people from dying of starvation — and as such are a humane solution to a desperate situation - but they do not eliminate poverty. Thus the government's remedial approach is unsound for the long term, when it does not coexist with programs that combat poverty at the root. Ultimately the misguided appropriation of benefits depletes the national budget and weakens its capability to sustain progress in the region.

Some private groups are now making strides to promote philanthropy. One such group is Zagros TV, which airs Charity and Joy, a show that allows guests to make a public plea for financial assistance. The pleas range from asking for help to finance medical treatment to gathering funds to repair decrepit homes. The program has helped numerous families cope with emergency situations, but unfortunately it does not solve their problems since urgent charity does not stop the cycle of poverty.

During my time in Kurdistan I sought the street beggars people complained about. I found them at work in certain areas of Erbil province. For many reasons — including their general caution — it was difficult to establish communication with these unconventional workers. I remember one girl in particular, no older than 13, who sat before a few soap bars neatly displayed on the ground. She remained quiet and still, as her eyes dashed in every direction, eagerly hoping for a customer. This girl is the typical Erbil beggar — one who sells small objects, often for personal use, in return for petty cash. However, most passing people tend to give charitable cash to these beggars and do not collect the items on sale.

People who have never begged seldom perceive begging as work, and consequently regard beggars with scorn and distrust. I remember one incident that illustrates how this detached attitude can manifest cruelly. It happened when I was visiting my grandmother in Kurdistan on the eve of Ramadan (a period that requires Muslims to fast from sunrise to sundown during the ninth month of the Islamic calendar year). We had been sitting in the family room when an urgent knock on the front door interrupted the evening. When my cousin opened the door she found a slender woman holding a small child. Islamic teachings advise Muslims to heed pleas for help, particularly when such arrive at one's home, so we were honoured to respect the tradition. "Helat" was the woman's name and "Fatima" was her four-year-old daughter. The child was disheveled, her cheeks bore the faint marks of sunburns. Her clothes were soiled and the sandals on her tiny feet missed several straps, exposing her flesh to the night air. How many eyes before mine had seen Fatima on these night journeys? How did she — at such an innocent age — view the world through the crippling lens of poverty? Questions continued to flood my mind in a courting dance with sadness.

Local activists have collected evidence showing that in some cases husbands force their wives and children to solicit charity at private homes. The activity has added to the public's contempt for beggars, and lowered their chances of receiving help. This outcome pushes poor children further into an isolating poverty fraught with parental neglect and increased emotional trauma — which comes when they witness their mothers beg in hostile environments.

DRIVING IN ERBIL

"The total ugliness and indifference of the worst features of the human race come out in their driving habits."

Charles Bukowski

People who learned to drive outside of Kurdistan might want to consider thinking twice before they drive in Erbil. The area's motorists have a unique driving style characterised by unpredictable manoeuvres fit to frighten Formula One drivers. With this in mind, I sought a local teacher who could train me to join the legion of road mavericks. He said this would require 15 lessons, each lasting 40 minutes, at the "good price" of US$130. The initial lessons would leave me with plenty to remember that Kurdistan is not Britain and my dual heritage predisposes me to cultural comedy. On the day of the first lesson I awoke early, ironed my clothes and polished my shoes in preparation for the excitement ahead. The instructor and I had agreed on 10 a.m. as the meeting time, but the hour passed with no sign of him. When I reached him via mobile, he said he was on his way to meet me, and sure enough his car appeared near the house. I ran outside and entered the vehicle with excitement. He took the wheel first, driving on a nearby road of two lanes. Then it was my turn to take the driver's seat. I made a move to adjust the mirrors, so that I could ensure a clear view of the rear, but the instructor said "Don't bother, they are fine." They were not however, because I am short and could not see the reflections without raising my body from the seat — which should obviously not be done while driving. I buckled my seat belt and waited for the instructor to inquire about my eyesight, but he did not. "That pedal moves the car," he declared, pointing to the accelerator near my foot. The man spent the next moments proudly enunciating the names of car parts. When I pressed the accelerator he urged caution even though we had barely moved. I surrendered to explosive laughter, which my instructor met with visible discontent. His annoyed expression made the situation more comical and I struggled to follow his commands while enduring a serious fit of the giggles.

During my driving apprenticeship in Kurdistan, my master punctuated the lessons with "He's driving illegally!" and "That's an illegal turn!" exclamations. This humoured me at first, but by the third lesson I had joined him in a chorus of outraged vocalisations. I lost count of how many times cars turned abruptly before us, and pedestrians walked onto roads — with an entitled air — as if courting disaster. When he tired of this circus my instructor moved the lessons to a deserted road riddled with rocks — all conspiring to jump in my direction as I piloted the car. "You need to pay attention!" he cautioned each time the front tires bumped a large rock. After feeling the reverberations of each collision, I wondered why I was driving on a road with more obstacles than a safari path. The question seemed particularly relevant in light of the fact that I had learned to drive years earlier in London.

Nevertheless the training delivered: by the last lesson I had embraced speed with newfound Kurdish bravery.

The business of driving lessons is a relatively new venture in Southern Kurdistan. Previously, in the past decade or so people learned the craft from relatives, but increased modernisation in the region has created a growing demand for formalised instruction. This has given rise to a new market of mobile driving schools, paved by instructors who set the rules on the road. For its part, the regional government sets an age limit for the operation of vehicles, and penalises those caught violating regulations, but people with powerful connections often escape punishment.

BACK TO LONDON

September is near and it is time for my return to
London. I am torn between leaving Kurdistan and
returning to the place I have called home for half of
my life. The ride to the airport is bittersweet,
marked by sadness and excitement. Parts of the road
fall from sight into the backdrop as the car conquers
each mile, and with them nestles my heart in the
mounds of this beautiful land. I open the window
and the distinctive scent of dry terrain consoles my
soul. A nostalgic screen appears before my eyes, in
the style of near afterlife slides, with the story of my
summer adventure. It features people I love and
people I do not understand and people who mystify
me — some of them stars in all three categories.
Suddenly the bright lights of a bustling city pierce

through the image, and London comes into focus, claiming the spotlight. We arrive at the designated terminal and outside stands an airplane whose wings extend beyond the Middle Eastern tarmacadam. I feel infinitely happy.

"No matter what you do, the UK will never be your homeland," a friend informed me in 2009. The comment was hurtful, but mostly unconvincing because it lacked logical sense. Such pronouncements do not seduce me because I am optimistic and understand that humanity is greater than territorial borders or ethnic characteristics. I believe that the scope of human existence and benevolence can extend beyond societal delineations. Thus a Russian millionaire may want to feed 1,000 families in rural Kenya just as a Norwegian teacher might help educate young men in a South African township. The point is that it matters not where need lies, but whether we seize the open invitation to help improve conditions for other human beings. Kurdistan is one of these places, where the alarm sounds loud and clear. Poor people in this area — particularly women and children — balance their lives on a thin wire pulled by devastation and injustice. To help them we do not need Kurdish ancestry or a desire to blame the inherently corrupt system that has failed them; we need vision, organisation, capital and an unshakable commitment to justice.

The magnificent view from above the Citadel of Erbil reminds me that the area is ripe for change in both tangible and cultural landscapes. I see great promise in the region, and I have begun to work with local organisations to inspire a culture of voluntarism among young people. Volunteer work and camaraderie will help them discover the seeds of unity that move nations forward.

Kurdistan has powerful people willing to engineer social and political change. Many of them have offered moral and logistical support to me at crucial junctures. My call to bring attention to Kurdistan began with a laptop and an open heart, but during the course of my exploration I encountered others moved by mutual concern. I now understand that I am not alone in my quest to help. There are countless others wanting to steer Kurdistan in the direction of progress, to a place of balanced possibility, where power and greed never drown humanity.

There are men and women in the region whose concern for the environment motivates them to reassess old systems that compromise our health and ecosystems. New leaders have begun to demonstrate concern for the impoverished areas of Kurdistan. They express a keen desire to see young people learn that the path to education is universal. These small steps help Kurdistan bask under a promising limelight.

ABOUT THE AUTHOR

Ruwayda Mustafah Rabar (Born 1989, Kurdistan, Erbil) is a British-Kurdish activist, blogger and law graduate from Kingston Law School. She has obtained Masters with commendation in International Political Communication and is currently completing her PhD at Kingston University.

Made in the USA
Middletown, DE
16 May 2017